A GUIDE TO FORMATION ADVISING
FOR SEMINARY FACULTY

A COMPANION TO
A Guide to Formation Advising for Seminarians
by Deacon Edward J. McCormack

A Guide to Formation Advising for Seminary Faculty

Accompaniment, Participation, and Evaluation

Deacon Edward J. McCormack

FOREWORD BY
RONALD D. WITHERUP, PSS

The Catholic University of America Press

Washington, DC

Copyright © 2020 by Edward J. McCormack
The Catholic University of America Press
All rights reserved

Library of Congress Cataloging-in-Publication data

Names: McCormack, Edward J., 1960- author.
Title: A guide to formation advising for seminary faculty : accompaniment, participation, and evaluation / Deacon Edward J. McCormack ; foreword by Ronald J. Witherup, PSS.
Description: Washington, DC : The Catholic University of America Press, 2020. | Includes bibliographical references and index. | Summary: "Recent Vatican guidelines for seminary formation call for professional accompaniment of seminarians throughout their formation to become Catholic priests. This book explains in concrete detail how to do this through the entire formation process. Written by a veteran formator at a Roman Catholic seminary, it offers a practical guide to formation advising as a ministry of accompaniment, participation, and evaluation. Formators will also find explanation of the evaluation process with a style sheet and examples of written evaluations. The handbook contains an index and an annotated bibliography on all the major topics a formation advisor comes across"— Provided by publisher.
Identifiers: LCCN 2020024231 | ISBN 9780813233130 (paperback) | ISBN 9780813233147 (ebook)
Subjects: LCSH: Catholic Church—Clergy—Training of. | Catholic theological seminaries. | Priesthood—Catholic Church. | Pastoral theology—Catholic Church.
Classification: LCC BX903 .M328 2020 | DDC 282.071/1—dc23
LC record available at https://lccn.loc.gov/2020024231

*To the present and former faculty and seminarians
of Theological College in Washington, DC.*

You give me hope for the future of the Church.

Contents

Acknowledgments xi
Foreword *by Ronald D. Witherup, PSS* xiii

Introduction 1

1. Understanding the Process of Formation 7
    The Stages of Priestly Formation 8
    Four Dimensions of Formation 10
    Four Characteristics of Formation 13
    General Principles of Formation 15
    A Christocentric and Trinitarian Spirituality 17
    The Context(s) of Formation 18
    The Formator 23

2. Formation Advising 29
    Two Forms of Accompaniment 29
    What is Formation Advising? 32
    Accompaniment: A Caring Approach 36
    Attachments 38
    What are the Essential Skills of Accompaniment? 41
    Intercultural Communication 51

Accompanying Seminarians throughout the Year   53
Formation Issues throughout the Four Years
of Formation   56

3. Formation Advising and the Gift of Accompaniment   63
Introducing a Seminarian to Formation Advising   64
Accompaniment: Getting to Know a Seminarian   68
Accompaniment: Understanding His Vocation Story and His
Call to Chaste Celibacy   75
Accompaniment: Human Formation Issues   81
Accompaniment: Priestly Ministry Skill Development   88
Accompaniment: Discipleship and Conformity to Christ
the Shepherd and Servant   90
Conclusion   95

4. Forming of the Heart and the Imagination   97
Deeper Listening: The Heart and the Imagination   98
The Deep World Within   107
Implications for Formation   117
Accompaniment and Deep Listening   119

5. The Power of Participation   125
Fostering a Growth Mindset   126
The Practice of Regular Reflection   130
Preparing for Formation Advising Meetings   132
Formation Goal Setting Process   133
Reflection on Pastoral Practice   136
Reflection on Preaching   138
The Annual Seminarian Self-Evaluation   139
Conclusion   140

6. Evaluations   141
   Bias in the Evaluation Process   142
   Fall Review   146
   Pre-Evaluation Conversation   147
   Guiding the Seminarian's Self-Evaluation   149
   Writing the Seminarian's Annual Evaluation   150
   Faculty Evaluation Style Sheet   151
   Sample Evaluation   152
   More Sample Evaluations   159

Selected Bibliography   183
Index   203

Acknowledgments

DURING MY TWENTY YEARS as a professor of theology and a formation advisor, so many people have been generous to me and supportive of my work and career. I want to thank Robert Leavitt, PSS, who hired me to be a member of the faculty at St. Mary's Seminary and University while I was still completing my dissertation. It was there that I first learned about formation advising. Phillip J. Brown, PSS, supported this project from its inception. I am grateful to Gerald McBrearity, the Rector of Theological College who has supported this project from beginning to completion. Gerry, David Thayer, PSS, and Jim Froelich, OFM, Cap. All read early drafts of the manuscript and provided critical comments that improved the work immensely. Richard Gula, PSS, read through a draft of the manuscript offering careful and critical comments. I am grateful to the time and care he took in reading the entire draft. I have learned so much about forming men for the priesthood from the faculty at Theological College and the many seminarians I have had the privilege of work with over these many years. They give me hope for the future of the Church. I want to thank John Martino and Catholic University of America Press for their support and guidance throughout this project. Finally, I want to thank my wife and two girls for their presence, support, and love. They make all the work worthwhile.

Foreword

POPE FRANCIS HAS A knack for soundbites. In November 2015, speaking on the 50th anniversary of Vatican Council II's documents on priestly ministry, life, and formation, the Holy Father made the acute observation: "Priests also have a history, they are not 'mushrooms' which sprout up suddenly in the cathedral on the day of their ordination." The expression alludes to the fact that priests must be formed. They do not arrive at the altar to be ordained without proper cultivation, that is, formation in all its dimensions.

Priestly formation, however, is not self-evident. It remains one of the most challenging ministries in the Church today. This is true not only because of the complex nature of the ministry itself, but also because the changing circumstances of formation programs today require a much more refined approach to formation than in the past. Knowledge of human, spiritual, ecclesial, psychological, and pastoral dimensions of priestly formation is needed. Ordination itself does not equip a priest to become a formator. Formation is both an art and an acquired skill, one that benefits greatly from experienced formators who have accumulated wisdom during their personal ministry. Just as spiritual direction, in the internal forum, is crucial in priestly formation, so is "formation advising," which happens in the external forum and thus bears the onus for recommending a candidate for Holy Orders.

This book is a tool to help formators in their specialized ministry. I am pleased to recommend it as a resource for formators, whether new or experienced, who are looking for clear guidance in formation advising. It is shaped by a Sulpician pedagogy rooted in centuries of priestly formation, and its approach is a reliable model for other programs of priestly formation. It is thoroughly based upon the Church's most recent official teachings on priestly formation, particularly *Pastores Dabo Vobis* (1992) and the revised universal norms expressed in the *Ratio Fundamentalis Formationis Sacerdotalis* (2017). The former document, promulgated by Pope Saint John Paul II, grew out of a worldwide synod of bishops that addressed modern, post-conciliar questions of priestly formation. The latter document, published by the Congregation for the Clergy after a broad worldwide consultation on the theme, is the standard universal program of priestly formation. Each national or regional conference of bishops must refer to it as they design local programs. Both of these documents provide a well-rounded approach, emphasizing the four main dimensions of priestly formation—human, spiritual, intellectual, and pastoral. All four dimensions must be addressed adequately, and in a synthetic, progressive, and integral manner. This book implements this same approach, with an emphasis on "unpacking" the implications of each step of priestly formation as the seminarian grows in the "gift" of his vocational identity.

A distinct advantage of this book is that it not only expresses well the theoretical foundations of priestly formation but also provides concrete models to follow. It gives helpful advice on assisting seminarians to take appropriate initiative for their own formation (*Ratio* §130) and to enter openly and freely into the discernment process. It also shows the importance of both communal and personal accompaniment, avoiding an over-reliance on only individual aspects of formation. An added bonus is a useful bibliography of other resources to consult.

On behalf of the General Council of the Society of the Priests of Saint Sulpice, I congratulate Deacon Edward McCormack for drawing on his great storehouse of psychological and ministerial know-how to produce this useful handbook that serves as a vital formational tool. May it provide future generations of formators with encouragement and hope as they go about their ministry.

Ronald D. Witherup, PSS, STL, PhD
Superior General
Society of the Priests of Saint Sulpice
Paris, 9 October 2019

Introduction

WELCOME TO THE MINISTRY of forming men for the diocesan priesthood. This ministry involves accompanying men through all the twists and turns of seminary formation. You will walk with them as they transition into seminary, grow in self-knowledge, wrestle with theology, learn to preach, and become a public leader and servant of God's people. While formation work is not often a person's first choice of ministry, it is a deeply rewarding ministry. The rewards come from knowing you are about God's work and making an impact on the future of the Church. It comes from getting to know the men whom you accompany through the formation process, watching them mature, gain clarity about their vocation, and develop pastoral skills needed to serve the people of God. Working as part of a formation faculty that shares a common vision and commitment about formation and cares and supports each other also makes this work meaningful. At the same time, this is a challenging ministry. It is more an art and spiritual practice than a science. It requires a formator to know himself well, maintain a robust prayer life, have a solid understanding of theology, know some psychology, and appreciate the practicalities of parish ministry.

The work of forming men for the priesthood is a behind-the-scenes ministry. When the people of God hear a priest preach, find him visiting their mother in the hospital, or offer them comfort and wisdom, they are encountering an ordained priest who has completed seminary formation. They know him as a good listener, a prayerful presider at liturgy, or a powerful preacher who can connect God's Word to their lives. What they do not see are the many years of formation and all the work that went into training this man into a healthy and holy priest. Nor are they aware of the formation team that makes much of this possible. But this "hidden ministry" is essential to the future of the Church, especially to parish life as so many people leave the Church after the recent sex abuse crisis and wonder if a priest can be trusted again.

The ministry of formation advising is also crucial to the success of each seminarian as he makes his way through the formation process. Seminary formation can be a very challenging experience. Most men come to seminary with a carload of unquestioned assumptions about God, prayer, Church, and priesthood. It can be unsettling and disorienting to have these assumptions challenged by their course of study, by spiritual directors, formation advisors, ministry experiences, and their fellow seminarians. This disorienting process often calls for a radical reorientation of many aspects of a person's life. He will need to grow in self-knowledge. Often long-standing psychological wounds will need to be healed. He will need to reconfigure his experience and understanding of God and to develop new interpersonal and ministerial skills.

Communal and personal accompaniment are necessary for a man to navigate this process successfully. A seminarian needs the support of family, friends, the bishop, his vocation director, and the entire seminary community. In the seminary, he is accompanied through the formation process by the seminary community, and especially seminary faculty, and by the rector, his spiritual director and formation advisor. This handbook seeks to explain the role the formation advisor plays in the formation process.

Why write a book on the ministry of formation advising? The reason is simple: Most people who are asked to participate in formation work lack the specialized training and skill development that are needed for this important and complex ministry. With some training in theology and parish ministry, they are asked to serve in the strange and complex world of formation ministry. What exactly is formation? How does formation occur? What kinds of knowledge, experience, and skills are needed to properly accompany a person through seminary formation? When I began this ministry fifteen years ago, I had no idea what I was getting into and what kinds of skills and knowledge I needed. I came to formation work with a Ph.D. in Systematic Theology and years of teaching experience, but little knowledge of what formation work entailed. Over the years, as I learned from experienced formators, I compiled notes for myself and developed handouts explaining the formation and evaluation process. When I noticed new colleagues struggling to understand what to do in advising meetings and how to write evaluations, I began to distribute my notes to them. They found the notes very helpful. That is the origin of this handbook.[1]

This handbook was written with first-time formation advisors in mind. It provides a comprehensive introduction to the ministry of formation advising with a focus on forming men in seminary for the diocesan priesthood. Chapter One sets out the process of formation and the contexts within which it occurs and identifies the basic characteristics and dimensions of formation work. In Chapter Two, I discuss the kinds of skills and practices required for this ministry. Chapter Three presents formation advising as the practice of accompanying a seminarian through the formation process. I describe what it means to accompany a seminarian through the major areas of formation, including discernment of his vocation, human formation issues, pastoral formation, and the major transition periods in seminary. Chapter Four describes the work of formation as a matter of transforming the heart, desires, and imagination

---

1. The approach to formation I present in this handbook draws on three main sources. First, I consider recent magisterial teaching on formation for ordained priesthood. This includes St. John Paul II's *Pastores Dabo Vobis* (Washington, D.C., Office for Publishing and Promotion Services, United States Catholic Conference, 1992), (hereafter, PDV), The *Program of Priestly Formation* (NCCB Publishing: 5th edition. September 2006), (hearafter PPF), the Congregation for the Clergy's recent publication *Ratio Fundamentalis Institutionis Sacerdotalis* (December 8, 2016), (hereafter, *Ratio*). Secondly, I have learned a great deal about formation from the approach to formation adopted by the Sulpician Fathers. The Sulpicians, founded by Father Jean Jacques Olier, are a society of priests whose sole mission is to form men for the priesthood. Finally, I also draw from the field of social psychology and positive psychology and its application to formation particularly as it is presented in executive coaching.

of the seminarian so that he embodies the heart of Christ the Good Shepherd. It considers the deeper dynamics at work in the formation process and the implicit questions formation work poses such as: What are we doing when we form men for the priesthood? How do we change a man's heart and mind into the heart and mind of Christ the Good Shepherd? In practical terms, what should a formator pay attention to as he meets with a seminarian? Chapter Five discusses the importance of seminarian participation in the formation process. It offers a variety of strategies for moving the seminarian to take responsibility for his formation. Chapter Six addresses the spring evaluation process. I offer guidelines for the seminarian's self-evaluation as well as a style sheet and guidelines for writing seminarian evaluations. Sample evaluations for each year in the formation process are provided. Finally, an annotated bibliography provides a list of books and articles on formation for the formator as well as a list of books, articles, and videos the formator can share with seminarians related to every formation topic.

1 | Understanding the Process of Formation

ANYONE NEW TO THE MINISTRY of forming men for the ordained priesthood can, at first, find it a challenging and confusing experience. You were once a seminarian and now you are a formator meeting with seminarians, attending faculty meetings, speaking with vocation directors, and writing evaluations. Like a person sailing a small boat in a vast ocean where large vessels and land masses suddenly appear and storms can pop up, a person will wonder, "What am I doing?" and "Where am I going?" This chapter gives the new formation advisor an overview of the various dimensions of the formation process. I describe the four stages and dimensions of formation, the characteristics of the formation process, and some general principles of formation, as well as identify the major agents and contexts of formation. I conclude the chapter by highlighting Christ as the formator and four fundamental features of priestly formation that have emerged in recent years.

The Stages of Priestly Formation

Seminary formation is a complex process that trains men for priestly life and parish ministry. This process is based on recent magisterial teaching regarding priestly identity and mission.[1] The identity of the priest is found in his conformity to Christ as Head, Shepherd, Servant, and Spouse. His mission is to serve the people of God in the parish by presiding at liturgy, proclaiming the Word, offering the sacraments, leading his people into the mystery of God, and guiding the parish in its participation in the mission of Christ. For a man to develop this identity and fulfill this mission, he needs formation.

The recent *Ratio* divides the process of formation into four stages: (1) A propaedeutic stage, (2) the discipleship stage, (3) the configuration stage, and (4) the pastoral stage. While each stage in the process has specific goals, the entire process is integrative with one stage building on and included in the next. The process of formation is more of a spiral than a straight line. A word about each stage can orient a formator to the overall approach to formation promoted by the Church.[2]

During the propaedeutic stage, formators provide seminarians with a solid basis for the spiritual life while nurturing

---

1. This includes Vatican Council II, *Lumen gentium*, especially no. 28; Vatican Council II, *Optatam totius*; *Pastores Dabo Vobis*; the most recent edition of the *Program of Priestly Formation*; and the Congregation for the Clergy's recent document *Ratio Fundamentalis* entitled *Gift of the Priestly Vocation*. This is not the place for a full theological exposition on the meaning of the priesthood; rather, I highlight the important features of priestly identity mentioned in *Lumen gentium*, *Pastores Dabo Vobis*, and the new *Ratio* as the basis for understanding the purpose of diocesan priestly formation.

2. *Ratio*, 59–63

self-awareness for personal growth. Seminarians are introduced to the Liturgy of the Hours, make regular use of the sacraments, become familiar with the Word of God, silence, prayer, and spiritual reading.[3]

Throughout the discipleship stage, formators work to form seminarians into disciples of Christ. All possible effort must go into training a seminarian to walk with Christ, to follow him, and get to know the Lord particularly through the Word.[4] In addition, a great emphasis is placed on human formation during this stage. The holiness of the priest is built upon it and depends on it. As the *Ratio* makes clear, "the importance of human formation cannot be sufficiently emphasized."[5]

The configuration stage acts as the conclusion to the discipleship stage by concentrating on conforming the seminarian to Christ the Shepherd and Servant. This demands that the seminarian devote himself to contemplating the person of Jesus Christ so he develops an intimate and personal relationship with the Lord.[6]

The pastoral formation stage occurs throughout the discipleship and configuration stages by gradually introducing the seminarian to various aspects of ministry with an eye towards ordination and priestly ministry in the parish.[7]

---

3. *Ratio*, 59.
4. *Ratio*, 62.
5. *Ratio*, 63.
6. *Ratio*, 68.
7. *Ratio*, 57.

Four Dimensions of Formation

Ever since the publication of *Pastores Dabo Vobis*, formators have spoken about the process of formation using the language of the four "pillars" of formation. The new *Ratio* has replaced the term "pillars" with the term "dimensions." The image of "pillars," while helpful for identifying the four features of formation, nevertheless failed to express the integrated relationship among the four dimensions of formation and seemed to imply that they were external to the seminarian. The language of "dimensions" holds on to the distinctive nature of each feature of the formation process while expressing the dynamic and inherently interdependent and relational nature of the four features of the formation process. Each dimension of formation interacts simultaneously with the others and aims to transform the seminarian's heart into the image of the heart of Christ the Good Shepherd.[8] I will highlight those aspects of each dimension of formation that *Ratio* views as important.

Human Dimension

Human formation is the foundation for all priestly formation since God calls concrete human beings to priestly ministry.[9] By privileging human formation, a seminary will promote the integral growth of every dimension of the person including physical health, psychological maturity, and the mature capacity for relationships with men and women.

---

8. *Ratio*, 89 quoting from *Optatam totius*, 4 and 19.
9. *Ratio*, 63, and 94.

Human formation fosters emotional maturity, an ability to be at ease with himself and others, a sense of responsibility, creativity, and a spirit of initiative. To achieve this kind of integral growth, a seminarian will need to develop self-knowledge and self-awareness. This occurs as he comes to understand his story, his gifts, and his weaknesses while learning to integrate these under the influence of the Holy Spirit. Community life, ministry, and his relationship to the formators, spiritual director, and formation advisor all play a role in human formation. For those dealing with problematic issues that stem from their family of origin or other life experiences, psychological counseling will be very beneficial.[10]

Spiritual Dimension

Spiritual formation aims to promote and nourish the seminarian's relationship with God and with all God's people in friendship with Jesus Christ in the power of the Holy Spirit. Growing in union with Jesus Christ is a purifying and transformative experience that is manifest in generous and sacrificial love. It should inform all pastoral ministry experiences. Spiritual growth requires participating in daily Eucharist, praying the Liturgy of the Hours, taking advantage of the sacrament of Penance, sustaining spiritual direction, making an annual retreat, silent prayer, and developing a devotion to Mary and the saints. A special emphasis must be given to chaste celibacy and the seminarian's relationship to the Word of God.[11]

---

10. *Ratio*, 94–95.
11. *Ratio*, 101–03.

Intellectual Dimension

Intellectual formation aims to develop the seminarian's knowledge of Scripture and his understanding of our theological traditions. His studies should impact his human, spiritual, and pastoral formation but more often than not, formation advisors will have to help seminarians make these connections. Theological studies should provide a seminarian with the ability to proclaim the Gospel in a way that is credible, captivating, and challenging. At the same time, they should allow him to dialogue with the contemporary world. He should be able to hear, distinguish, and interpret the many voices in our day in the light of the Gospel. By integrating intellectual formation into the other dimensions of formation, the seminarian will develop into a priest who can serve and give witness to the Word in the Church and the world.[12]

Pastoral Dimension

The *Ratio* strongly encourages every dimension of seminary formation to be informed by a pastoral spirit. This dimension of formation challenges every seminarian to learn how to seek out, walk alongside, and lead the sheep in a spirit of compassion, generosity, and love. All pastoral ministry courses and all ministry experiences must promote the vision and practice of Christ the Good Shepherd. Pastoral formation involves developing pastoral ministry and leadership skills. It also calls for the development of the art and skill of preaching. In addition, the priest must become an

---

12. *Ratio*, 116–18.

expert in pastoral discernment where he listens deeply to the experience of the people, interprets situations with wisdom, and accompanies the people of God with love.[13]

Four Characteristics of Formation

Formation for priestly ministry requires that every seminarian participate fully in each dimension of the formation process. This process is marked by four characteristic elements: Discipleship, integration, community, and mission.

Discipleship

The process of forming priests follows the singular journey of discipleship that every Christian undergoes beginning with baptism and the sacraments of initiation. At the same time, it offers a seminarian an intensive form of this journey into discipleship as he comes to appreciate how this call to be a disciple of Jesus is at the center of his life and priesthood. It is a journey into the life of the Triune mystery that occurs through participation in the seminary community and through ministry, which will lead him to serve others in cooperation with Christ and the Spirit.[14]

Integration

Seminary formation, when done well, fosters the interaction and gradual integration of all four dimensions of formation

---

13. *Ratio*, 120.
14. *Ratio*, Introduction, 3.

in the life of the seminarian. The seminary should strive to maintain a balance among all four dimensions of formation. Certain formation experiences such as community life, hospital ministry, preaching, and leadership opportunities can function as key integrative experiences for the seminarian. Seminarians will often need help understanding how the four dimensions interact with each other. Formation advisors and spiritual directors must help them reflect on their experience so they begin to recognize when integration occurs and see how valuable it is to priestly life and ministry.[15]

Community

Formation for priesthood is communal in character. In our excessively individualistic culture, this may not be obvious to seminarians. Helping them to understand and value community is fundamental to the work of formation. Likewise, every formator must learn to consider himself part of a formative community. The seminarian comes from the Christian community to join a seminary community to be sent back to serve the Christian community in his diocese. He needs to be formed by the community and formed to lead and shepherd a community. His vocation is discovered and accepted within the people of God. It is formed within the context of the seminary community. In many seminaries, this is a multicultural and multiethnic experience.[16] In the communal life of the seminary, all four dimensions of formation come together and interact most regularly with each other. It is in

---

15. *Ratio*, 89, 92.
16. PPF, 271.

community that many of the important human formation issues can emerge and be addressed by formators.[17]

Mission

Finally, formation is missionary in character. The Christian community is gathered together by the Spirit to be sent on a mission. This missionary impulse belongs to the entire people of God with a special focus on caring for the poor, justice, and peace. This should be reflected in the kinds of ministries selected as part of the pastoral formation program. Seminarians, therefore, should be formed as missionary disciples since the goal all formation is mission.[18] Mission binds together and animates all four dimensions of formation. It may not be obvious to seminarians how human, spiritual, and intellectual formation relate to mission. These topics will need to be discussed in rector's conferences, in spiritual direction, and in formation advising.

General Principles of Formation

The approach to formation advising presented in this handbook assumes that a set of general principles are operative in the way the seminary approaches formation. These principles are found in the new *Ratio* and are consistent with the Sulpician Fathers' approach to diocesan seminary formation.[19]

---

17. *Ratio*, Introduction, 3, also see 90.
18. *Ratio*, Introduction, 3, 91.
19. The material for this section was taken from Ronald D. Witherup, PSS, ed., *The Sulpicians: A Tradition of Priestly Formation* (Society of Saint Sulpice, 2013). The Sulpician tradition of seminary formation traces its origins and inspiration to the

A Formative Community

The entire seminary community plays a central role in the formation process. All men and women who comprise the faculty contribute to the integral formation of priests. Furthermore, all aspects of community life impact the formation of men for the priesthood.

Collegiality

The formation faculty work together with an openness to the Holy Spirit to form men for the priesthood while modeling a spirit of collaboration for the seminarians.

Missionary and Apostolic Spirit

The seminary is a unique time in which a man is asked to deepen his experience of the Lord through study, prayer, community life, and ministry so that upon ordination he is filled with the Spirit and ready for priestly mission and ministry.

A Graduated and Adult Approach

Seminary formation works best when a graduated approach is adopted and the seminarians are treated as adults. A graduated approach to formation introduces different facets

---

founder of the Society of Saint Sulpice, Father Jean Jacques Olier (1608–1657), pastor of the Church of Saint Sulpice in Paris. Father Olier and his associates founded seminaries with a desire to provide spiritual leaders who would renew the Church in France at the time. Deeply rooted in the French School of Spirituality that arose in the seventeenth-century, the Sulpicians have a distinctive method of priestly formation.

of seminary formation at different stages while respecting the individual needs and growth of each seminarian. From pre-theology through to ordination each seminarian is met on the level of his own particular development in relationship to the four dimensions of formation with attention to his needs. Each seminarian is called to develop his own personal priestly identity as he conforms himself to Christ the Good Shepherd. By treating seminarians as adults, the seminary invites the seminarian to take personal responsibility for his formation. This creates a collaborative environment between the formation faculty and seminarians. It also prepares seminarians for the freedom and responsibility that comes with priestly life.

A Christocentric and Trinitarian Spirituality

Priestly formation is built upon and fosters a Christ-centered and Trinitarian Spirituality. This approach to the spiritual life is reflected in the liturgy and should inform all aspects of a seminarian's human, spiritual and pastoral formation. Priestly formation then becomes a powerful participation in the life of Christ as the seminarian learns to discern and cooperate with the action of the Holy Spirit.

Union with Christ

All aspects of priestly formation must promote a close relationship with Jesus Christ, the Good Shepherd.

Emphasis on Word and Sacrament

Scripture and the Eucharist are central to seminary formation since both draw a seminarian closer to Christ and keep alive his interior life.

Love of the Church and the Priesthood

The goal of formation is to produce holy priests and effective pastors who are able and ready to lead in the contemporary Church.

Priestly Marian Piety

Mary functions as the perfect model for priesthood. Like Mary, every priest must hear the Word of God and keep it. Like her, his entire life must be marked by an ever-deepening union with Jesus her Son.

Spiritual Direction

Following the Sulpician tradition, priestly formation should hold to a strict distinction between the external forum and internal forum. The external forum deals with public knowledge, whereas the intern forum calls for absolute confidentiality in spiritual direction.

The Context(s) of Formation

The formation process I have been describing takes place within a variety of contexts where the various agents of formation operate.[20] These contexts can be pictured as a series of concentric circles that move from the outer circle to the inner circle. The outer circle consists of our contemporary culture and society; the next circle includes the bishop and diocese a seminarian comes from; the next circle contains the seminary community, the formation faculty, and finally the relationship between the formator and seminarian.[21] I offer a word about each of these contexts and their impact on formation.

Cultural and Historical Contexts

Formation for the ministerial priesthood takes place within a variety of cultural contexts.[22] By culture, I mean the practices and behaviors that a society and community engage in including language, food, dress, or the way we greet a person. What inspires these practices are the stories, symbols, and beliefs that are foundational to the society. The various cultural contexts where formation takes place include the culture of the country where the seminary is found, the culture of the sending diocese, and the culture of the seminary itself.

Formation today is also conducted in settings where a mix of cultures interact with each other, whether it be the seminary, the parish, or the diocese. Such a multicultural environment means cultural, linguistic, and economic

---

20. The various agents of formation include the diocesan bishop, the presbyterate where the seminarian comes from, the community of formators, and the seminarian himself.

21. *Ratio*, 139.

22. See *Building Intercultural Competence for Ministers* (United States Conference of Catholic Bishops, 2014).

diversity within a diocese, seminary, and parish. These situations often involve a clash of different practices and behaviors driven by different beliefs and values. Formators need to be aware of these cultural and historical factors that shape a seminarian's life and help him negotiate them.[23]

What complicates things even more is that every culture, as well as every institution and community, has a history that continues to develop and change. Cultural practices and beliefs come from somewhere and are going somewhere. Formation happens at a moment within the history of the universal Church. It takes place within the historical context of the diocese. Every seminary has a history and a culture. This history is shaped by the current and past rectors, and the makeup of the faculty, the student body, and the relationship the seminary has with the local ordinary. The approach to formation adopted by a seminary and how it is received by a seminarian are the result of historical and cultural developments.

---

23. My discussion of history, society, and culture is shaped by Bernard Lonergan's concept of the Scale of Values found in *Method in Theology* (Toronto: University of Toronto Press, 1971). By historical context, I mean the changes and developments that occur over time in a given society and culture. The social context refers to the various interpersonal and communal relationships including friends, family, neighborhoods, and Church communities and the different economic, political, and technological institutions that are meant to serve those communities. By culture, I mean an assumed set of meanings and values that are expressed in practices and various artistic forms both in classic cultural venues and through popular culture. In a given society there is a dominant culture and various subcultures that are often in conflict with each other. The values and meanings of any culture are promoted through cultural and communal practices, and political and institutional policies, including education and religion. The various cultural values and meanings found in a given society often conflict with each other. The influence that historical developments and cultural trends have on formation is a complex and multidimensional subject that warrants study on the part of the formator but is beyond the scope of this book. The bibliography offers directions for further study in this area.

To be a bit more concrete, consider some of the recent historical and cultural factors in the United States that influence priestly formation today. We live in a diverse, multicultural, ecumenical, and interreligious society that is constantly changing. Within the Church, the sexual abuse crisis, the priest shortage, the multicultural make-up of our parishes, the many Catholics who are leaving our Church today, and the growing number of unchurched are all part of our context. Some of the chief cultural factors that influence seminarians and formators alike are: American individualism;[24] a dominant culture that dismisses Christianity as irrelevant to the real concerns of the world;[25] the all-pervasive presence of pornography on the internet; and the ways social media impact how people converse and relate to each other.[26] These are just a few examples. I encourage formators to stay abreast of these influences and be aware of how they impact the formation process. A section of the bibliography that accompanies this handbook offers suggestions for further reading on these issues.[27]

---

24. Robert Bellah, Richard Madsen, William M. Sullivan, Ann Swidler, and Steven M. Tipton, *Habits of the Heart: Individualism and Commitment in American Life* (University of California Press; third edition, 2007).

25. Ronald Rolheiser, ed, *Secularity and the Gospel: Being Missionaries to Our Children* (New York: The Crossroad Publishing Company, 2006); James K. A. Smith, *How (not) to be Secular: Reading Charles Taylor* (Grand Rapids: Eerdmans Publishing Company, 2014).

26. Sherry Turkle, *Reclaiming Conversation: The Power of Talk in a Digital Age* (New York: Penguin Press, 2015).

27. The PPF, 12–13, lists a number of significant features of life in the United States in the twenty-first century that includes secularity, the unchurched, the semi-active Catholic, our ecumenical and interreligious context, the cultural, linguistic, and economic diversity in the country and among seminarians.

Ecclesial Context

The ecclesial context of each seminarian plays a role in his experience of formation. Each seminarian is sponsored by a diocese with the support of the bishop and his vocation director. Each diocese has its own history, its own social, cultural, and economic makeup, and its own needs. Within a diocese, there are various social and cultural dynamics at work among the priests and people of a diocese that inform how priests relate to each other, the bishop, and the people. Even within a diocese, there can be a great deal of diversity around these factors. For instance, the social, economic, and cultural makeup of downtown Washington, D.C. is quite different from the rural life in southern Maryland. Formators need to take these factors into account when working with men from different dioceses.

Seminary Community

The seminary community is the dominant context within which the seminarian experiences his formation. Every seminary community has a history that is shaped by past and present rectors, faculty, and seminarians. Life in the seminary is shaped by the rector and his style of leadership, the Rule of Life and other policies and traditions that have developed over the history of the seminary. The quality of the faculty and the relationships within and among the formation faculty impact seminary life as does the caliber of the student body. These complex relationships are lived out in the daily and weekly routines and activities that make seminary life inside and outside the house.

The Relationship Between the Seminarian and the Formator

The last context to consider is the relationship between the seminarian and formator. This relationship can take the form of spiritual direction or formation advising. In each case, the seminarian and formator each brings to this relationship his own personal history, vocation story, educational experience, and spiritual journey. This relationship always takes place within the relationship Christ has with the seminarian and the formator.

The Formator

I conclude this overview of the formation process by saying a few words about the fundamental formator and four important features of formation that have emerged in recent years. Every seminarian and every person involved in forming men for the priesthood must remember that the formator guiding the entire seminary formation process is the risen Jesus. As the principal agent of priestly formation, the Lord works through the power of the Holy Spirit to influence every dimension of the process.[28] In *Pastores Dabo Vobis*, Pope John Paul II describes the central role Christ plays in the formation process this way:

> To live in the seminary, which is a school of the Gospel, means to follow Christ as the apostles did. You are *led by Christ* into the service of God the Father and of all

---

28. Ratio, 55.

people, under the guidance of the Holy Spirit. Thus you become more like Christ the good shepherd in order better to serve the Church and the world as a priest.[29]

The *Ratio* develops this insight further by instructing us that the "principal agent of priestly formation is the Most Holy Trinity."[30] The Triune mystery works to form seminarians through the presence of Christ and the many actions of the Holy Spirit. Through the power of the Holy Spirit, Christ is present to each seminarian in the community, in his proclaimed Word, in the sacraments, as well as in spiritual direction, formation advising, and every time seminarians participate in ministry. The Lord walks with the seminarian, guides him, and dwells in him through the process of formation. At the same time, the Lord walks ahead of the seminarian, always inviting him to become the person the Lord wants him to become.

The risen Jesus uses every dimension of seminary life to form men for the priesthood. He acts like a potter forming a man into a priest ready to serve God's people. At times the Lord will cut things out from a man's life; at other times, he introduces new gifts and abilities as he forms and shapes the seminarian. The entire seminary experience is designed to support this effort: liturgy, prayer, spiritual direction, philosophy and theology courses, formation advising, life in the house, relationships, and ministry. The potter uses the formation process to heal, free, reform, and reorient the man in the light of the Gospel. Formation, therefore, has a paschal

---

29. *PDV*, 42.
30. *Ratio*, 125.

or cruciform character to it. It challenges the seminarian to identify and rid himself of habits, attitudes, assumptions, and behaviors that prevent him from becoming an image of Christ the Shepherd and Servant. It also involves cultivating healthy and holy habits that allow Christ to shine through him in a unique way.

Let me conclude this overview to the formation process by highlighting four important features of that process that have emerged from recent magisterial teaching. The first is conviction that human formation is the foundation of all other dimensions of formation. Almost every person enters seminary carrying with him wounds received from his family of origin and life experience. He will also bring with him assumptions about himself and how to find meaning as well as distorted ways of behaving that are contrary to the Gospel. Human formation must be a top priority in the early years of formation. When these wounds and issues are not addressed, a priest can be a slave to them rather than a servant of Christ. It can undermine his relationship with Christ and with others and impact his ability to engage in pastoral ministry and pastoral leadership no matter how much he prays. The emphasis on human formation has taken on greater importance in recent years in the light of the sex-abuse scandal. It is also important as we see so many people leaving the Church because a priest was unkind, rude, or controlling rather than kind, loving, and free to let Christ work through him.

A second feature of seminary formation that deserves attention is the conviction that the priest is a lifelong disciple of Jesus.[31] Pope Francis reminds us that "formation…is an

---

31. *Ratio*, 54, 62.

experience of permanent discipleship, which draws one close to Christ and allows one to be ever more conformed to Him. Therefore, it has no end, for priests never stop being disciples of Jesus, they never stop following him."[32] All the baptized are called to live as disciples of Jesus within the life of the Church as she cooperates with the mission of Jesus.[33] The seminarian is a disciple who has discerned a call to live out his discipleship in public ordained service to the People of God. Seminary formation offers an intense training in discipleship where men are formed into visible signs of the merciful love of God the Father.[34] He will learn to participate in the saving work of Christ, especially as he offers the people of God the sacraments and provides pastoral care to them. This requires an understanding of the liturgy, the sacraments, and the development of pastoral skills. Every seminarian needs to discover the charisms God gives him to live out his priestly vocation. At the same time, he must be trained to discern the charisms the Holy Spirit gives the people in the parish so they can participate in the mission of the Church.[35]

A third feature worth highlighting is how the priest is called to conform himself to Christ as Head, Shepherd, Servant, and Spouse. Being conformed to Christ refers to the Holy Spirit's transformation of a priest's heart, mind, and imagination so that he is a unique expression of Christ's presence in the parish. It involves a cruciform process of the

---

32. Ratio 54, quoting Pope Francis, *Letter to Participants in the Extraordinary General Assembly of the Italian Episcopal Conference* (November 8, 2014: *L'Osservatore Romano* 258), 7.

33. *Ratio,* 57.

34. *Ratio,* 35.

35. *Ratio,* 31–32.

seminarian ridding himself of all behaviors, attitudes, and vices that are contrary to Christ while growing in union with Christ so that the Lord is the dominant influence in the life of the priest. Conformity to Christ also involves character development and the cultivation of Gospel virtues known as the fruits of the Spirit. The goal of character formation is always other directed—complete giving of oneself in tender love to the People of God.[36]

The final feature of formation, follows from the previous one and its implications for the model of leadership a pastor adopts in the parish. It is the close connection between the priest's conformity to Christ the Shepherd and Servant and how the priest relates to and leads the people of God. This relationship is characterized by loving service as an authoritative leader of the people, teacher of the Word, and minister of the sacraments.[37] By conforming himself to Christ the Shepherd, the priest will devote himself to gathering, accompanying, caring for, and leading his sheep. He will give special attention to the lost sheep.[38] He will adopt the model of servant leader that is expressed in joyful generosity and a freedom to put the needs of the other ahead of his own. This form of leadership is contrary to the popular forms that emphasize power, control, and prestige. It requires self-awareness and often a real conversion from power to service. He must become a man of discernment who lives from a high level of self-knowledge, a deep interior life, and

---

36. *Ratio*, 36–43.
37. *Ratio*, 33.
38. *Ratio*, 37.

a mature capacity to enter relationships with others.[39] This form of leadership calls for a transformation that renews the heart and mind of the person so that he can discern what is the will of God. In this way he will be able to choose, decide, and act according to the will of God."[40]

---

39. *Ratio*, 41.
40. *Ratio*, 43.

2 | Formation Advising

IN THE PREVIOUS CHAPTER, I offered an overview of the stages and dimensions of the formation process. In this chapter, I discuss the role of the formation advisor in the formation process. The primary role of the formation advisor is to personally accompany a seminarian through the formation process. I set out the basic approach to accompaniment, discuss the fundamental skills needed for formation advising, and conclude with a list of common formation issues that need to be addressed by the formation advisor throughout the academic year and through the course of formation.

Two Forms of Accompaniment

Most men who fully engage seminary formation find it to be an intense journey that reorients, renews, and transforms their hearts and minds. To successfully navigate this process, a man needs communal and personal accompaniment.[1] Communal accompaniment comes from living with fellow

---

1. *Ratio*, 44–52.

seminarians and resident faculty. It comes through participation in daily liturgy, communal prayer, various house committees, recreational activities, and the interpersonal relationships, exchanges and discussions that come with community living.[2] Seminarians also need to be accompanied in a personal way as they proceed through the various stages of formation.[3] The rector, close friends, spiritual direction, and formation advising offer a seminarian the personal accompaniment necessary to survive and thrive in seminary.

The two most common forms of personal accompaniment are spiritual direction and formation advising. There is an important difference between these two that is worth highlighting at this point in our discussion. According to a number of canons in the *1983 Code of Canon Law* spiritual direction in the seminary exists for the sake of the spiritual formation of candidates for the priesthood. It concerns the spiritual good and spiritual progress of the seminarian.[4] Traditionally, spiritual direction enjoys the highest degree of confidentiality such that nothing shared or uncovered in spiritual direction can ever be revealed to anyone under any circumstances. The reason for this is that spiritual direction is offered exclusively for the spiritual benefit and formation of the seminarian. For those working in a Sulpician seminary, there is a long tradition that equates the level of confidentiality found in the internal forum with the seal of Confession. In practical terms, this prevents the spiritual

---

2. *Ratio*, 50–52.
3. *Ratio*, 44.
4. *The Code of Canon Law* (London: Harper Collins, 1983), Canons 240, 244, 245, 246.

director from commenting on any of his current or former directees at a faculty meeting.

This is stated clearly by the PPF in the fourth edition in paragraph 483:

> *Since spiritual direction takes place in the internal forum, the relationship of seminarians to their spiritual director is a privileged and confidential one. Spiritual directors may not participate in the evaluation of those they presently direct or whom they directed in the past.*

The fifth edition to the PPF has caused some confusion about this long-standing tradition in paragraph 134 with the following line:

> *The only possible exception to this standard of confidentiality would be the case of grave, immediate, or mortal danger involving the directee or another person.*

This line has led to a great deal of confusion that is being debated by canon lawyers and formators. This handbook stands with the traditional practice and that of the Sulpician Fathers that awards the highest confidentiality to spiritual direction. The reason is that unless such a level of confidentiality is enjoyed in spiritual direction, the trust a seminarian places in his spiritual director will be eroded, thus undermining the spiritual benefit and formation potential of this fundamental relationship.

Formation advising, in contrast to spiritual direction, operates within the external forum. It includes discussions between the formation advisor and the seminarian and conversations with the formation faculty, the rector, the vocation director, and the bishop. It also includes meetings with vocation directors and seminarians. Formation advising enjoys a limited confidentiality. Although what is shared between the seminarian and advisor is not for public consumption and does not need to be shared with other faculty or vocation directors unless the matter is very serious, this confidentiality is limited because the advisor will, on occasion, inform the faculty of the seminarian's progress. Nevertheless, some level of confidentiality is necessary to build trust and honest rapport between the seminarian and his formation advisor. In such an atmosphere, formators can help seminarians discern their vocation and become aware of their gifts and weaknesses so they can be ever more receptive to God's grace.[5]

What is Formation Advising?

Formation advising is the prayerful and reflective practice of accompanying a seminarian through the formation process in the external forum. By accompanying a seminarian, the formator seeks to develop a relationship with him to know and understand the seminarian's life story, including his vocation story, interests, desires, and struggles. A formation advisor walks with a seminarian as he engages the four dimensions of formation to help the seminarian learn about himself and the ways Christ is trying to form him. A formator also seeks to understand how a seminarian is experiencing the various dimensions of formation—what he is

---

5. *Ratio*, 46–47.

learning, what is disturbing to him, and what is exciting and challenging to him. At times a formation advisor will offer a seminarian encouragement, feedback, and the occasional challenge. Through such a relationship, the formator can help the seminarian respond to God's call, understand his experience of formation, and grow into the priest Christ is calling him to become.

The approach to formation advising presented here is inspired by the way Jesus formed his disciples. After Jesus called Peter, James, Andrew, and John to follow him, he spent three years forming them into leaders of his mission. He walked with them, ate meals with them, taught them, and regularly invited them to share in his ministry. Sometimes the things Jesus said and did challenged them and even shocked them. Jesus knew these men came to him with their own life experiences, their own assumptions about God and the kingdom. He knew they had developed attitudes and behaviors that needed to be challenged and changed if they were to be his disciples and share in his ministry. Jesus knew each of these men in a personal way. He met them where they were and gave them what they needed at the time it was needed so they could grow into mature disciples. As Jesus walked through Galilee or ate meals, he listened to them and sought out ways to open their eyes to the vision of the kingdom of God. He worked to get them to see all God was doing so they could cooperate with the mission of the kingdom. He taught them the prayer of the kingdom. He taught them the virtues of the kingdom. Then he sent them out to share with others what they had learned and who they had become. It was their personal experience of

Jesus, their experience of the community of disciples Jesus was forming, the meals they shared with him, and the work they did on behalf of God's coming kingdom that formed them. Their formation reached a new level when Jesus was crucified, rose from the dead and appeared to them. Filled with the Spirit of God, aware of the presence of the risen Christ, and knowing God's new creation had dawned, they were ready to proclaim the good news, lead the Christian community, and go about the work of Christ.

This is how a formator should accompany a person through the formation process. Let me highlight the important dimensions of Jesus' approach to formation:

- He accompanied his disciples
- He knew them well
- He listened to them with care and compassion
- He called them to share in the coming kingdom of God
- He challenged them and changed their hearts and minds so they could cooperate with the kingdom
- He taught them about the vision and virtues of the kingdom of God
- He sent them out on mission and later listened to their experiences

New formators will find that formation advising is very complex and challenging work. Four factors contribute to the complexity and challenge of this work.

- First, every person who enters seminary brings with him his own life experience that includes the complex dynamics within his family of origin, his educational and work experience, a history of friendships and intimate relationships, and his own experience of God and vocational story. This history shapes every seminarian's view of himself and God. It informs how he relates to others and how he handles stress and conflict. It forms his assumptions about ministry, women, the Church, and the world. Some of these experiences and assumptions fit with the Gospel and some may be contrary to the Gospel. Formators spend time getting to know this history and its implications for the man he works with.

- A second factor is the structure of the formation program and the demands it makes on the seminarian. Each seminarian handles each stage in the process differently. A formator must know the various stages in the formation process, including the key events and expectations found at each stage. Likewise, he must understand the rhythm of the academic year and seminary calendar with its accompanying stresses and expectations such as midterms, evaluations, and liturgical events that mark the stages of formation.
- The third factor is the formator himself. Each formator brings his history, education, experience, and spiritual life to the process of accompanying men through formation. In addition, every formator brings strengths, gifts, weaknesses, and blind spots to the formation process. He must nourish and sustain his prayer life, his relationships, and his physical and mental health, and continue to develop virtues and skills needed for the ministry of formation advising.

- The final factor is that the mystery of God is present and at work in the life of the seminarian and the formator and in the formation advising experience. Layers of meaning and mystery are added to formation advising when we realize God is working within the seminarian and the formator and between them all the time.

Accompaniment: A Caring Approach

The relationship a formator seeks to develop with a seminarian as he accompanies him through the formation process needs to be based on trust and respect where the seminarian feels the care and concern of the advisor. When a seminarian begins to trust his formator, and believes he is safe and cared for, he will begin to let his defenses down and share what is really going on in his heart and mind. When that happens, real transformation can occur. To foster this kind of relationship a formation advisor must engage in the following intentional practices:

- Be present.
- Be attuned.
- Connect with the person.
- Forge a relationship built on trust and respect.[1]

A formator is present to a seminarian when he is open to whatever arises in himself and in the seminarian during the formation advising meeting. This requires being open to the

---

1. Daniel Siegel, *The Mindful Therapist* (New York: W. W. Norton & Company, 2010).

truth rather than to prior judgments. It means the formator is aware of the feelings and thoughts that come up in him while being open to feelings and thoughts the seminarian shares with him. Being present allows a formator to become attuned to what is going on with the person he works with.[2]

Being attuned means a formator understands what the seminarian is going through at this point in the formation process. A formator must be able to put aside his preoccupations, memories and judgments so he is receptive to what the seminarian is sharing with him and experiencing at this point in the semester. This requires an awareness of his eye contact, facial expressions, posture, and voice tone. When a formator is present to a seminarian and interested in his experience, the seminarian will feel "heard," "understood." He will sense that his formator cares about him and is interested in what he is feeling and thinking.[3]

A formator who is present and attuned to the seminarian will be able to engage him and connect with him in an interactive state known as "resonance." Resonance is the ability to feel what the other is feeling.[4] When a formator is open to the other and accepts what is shared and demonstrates genuine interest and care for a seminarian, trust emerges in the relationship. The first time most of us experience someone being attuned to our needs and feelings is with our parents. The attuned presence of a parent makes the vulnerable baby feel safe. Repeated experiences of attunement teach the child to trust that all will be well.

---

2. Siegel, *The Mindful Therapist*, 13–19 and 25–29.

3. Siegel, *The Mindful Therapist*, 34–40.

4. Siegel, *The Mindful Therapist*, 54–55 and 58–59.

When a formator is present and attuned to the seminarian, he will connect with him. He will understand what the man is feeling and experiencing.

Trust is a willingness to rely on others for connection, comfort, and protection. It is a feeling that says, "It is safe to be vulnerable with this person."[5] Trust allows a seminarian to be honest about his experience in formation and about his discernment. It creates an atmosphere where he can learn about his past and discover who God is calling him to be. Trust enables him to hear observations from the faculty about where he needs to grow as a seminarian and act on them.

Attachments

All relationships depend on the participation of each person in the relationship. How successful a formator will be at implementing these four steps to fostering a relationship with a seminarian will depend, to some extent, on whether or not the seminarian has what psychologists call a secure or insecure attachment. The terms secure or insecure attachments are drawn from the work of attachment theory, a theory well-known in the fields of psychology and social work. A brief summary of this theory can provide formators a way of understanding the impact a seminarian's family of origin has on how he relates to people in the present. This theory also offers formators insight into what each seminarian needs to work on in human formation.

In an ideal world, from the day we are born, our parents are present to us, attuned to our feelings and needs,

---

5. Siegel, *The Mindful Therapist*, 74–75.

and regularly connected with us so that a deep bond of trust grows between us. Unfortunately, different parenting styles lead to different experiences of attachment between a child and parent or caregiver. These childhood attachments shape relationships over the course of a lifetime.[6] The kind of attachment a child has depends on how consistently his or her parent was present, attuned, and connected to him or her as a child. Physical touch and other forms of human interaction are so crucial that research on infants in orphanages revealed reduced brain size and even death due to a lack of physical and emotional contact.[7] A person with a secure attachment grew up with a primary caregiver who, although not perfect, was consistently present and attuned to his or her needs. The child felt secure in the presence of this person. A person with a secure attachment has a concrete and detailed memory of his life story. He tends to make friends easily, knows how to relate to adults and copes well with stress.

Insecure attachments come in different forms with differing consequences. One kind of insecure attachment is called an avoidant attachment. A person with an avoidant attachment grew up with a primary caregiver who was emotionally withdrawn and psychologically unavailable to the child. This child learned to rely on himself or herself and did not develop close relationships with friends and adults. As an adult, he has a "dismissing" state of mind characterized by a

---

6. David Brooks, *The Social Animal: The Hidden Sources of Love, Character and Achievement* (New York: Random House Publishing, 2012), 61–63. The literature on attachment theory is massive. My goal is to alert the formator to its existence.

7. Thomas Lewis, MD et al, *A General Theory of Love* (New York: Random House Publishing, 2001), 67–70.

lack of details about past relationships, brevity of responses in conversations, and an insistence that his family had no impact on his development. When conversations turn to emotions, or when adults with avoidant attachment are asked to reveal themselves, they often react with unease. They tend to go through their days living within a narrow range of emotional reactions. The central theme of their adult life is "I am alone and relationships do not matter much." Such a person tends approach life from the perspective of linear and logical thinking. Developing the right hemisphere of the brain is important for integration.[8]

Another kind of insecure attachment is known as an ambivalent attachment. A primary caregiver tended to be inconsistent in the way he or she related to the child, shifting from being intrusive to being cold and aloof. As adults, they tend to be "preoccupied" by past issues and experiences that continually intrude on experiences in the present, often causing them to feel uncertain and anxious about relationships. They regularly feel they need others but cannot depend on them. Quite often, these insecurities originated with the caregiver but were internalized by the child and are now present in the adult.[9]

The good news coming from research on attachment theory is that persons raised with an insecure attachment can develop a secure attachment at a later point in life. This can happen if they have a relationship with a relative, neighbor, teacher, or counselor who is present to them, aware of how

---

8. Daniel J. Siegel, *Mindsight: The New Science of Personal Transformation* (New York: Bantam Books, 2010), 1 and 178.
9. Brooks, *The Social Animal*, 63–66.

they are feeling and interested in them so they connect with them. Under these conditions, they know they are safe. That kind of relationship gives the person the space and direction to make sense of his experience.[10] Formation advisors and spiritual directors are in a unique position to help move a person from an insecure attachment into a secure attachment. There are times, however, when professional counseling is also needed. More will be said about this below.

What are the Essential Skills of Accompaniment?

Every formation advisor will need to develop a set of skills to accompany a person through the formation process in a spirit of care and concern. The *Program of Priestly Formation* lists some of the important skills the advisor should employ.

> On every seminary faculty, certain members function as formators in the external forum. These formation advisors/mentors and directors should be priests. They *observe* seminarians and *assist* them to grow humanly by offering them *feedback* about their general demeanor, their relational capacities and styles, their maturity, their capacity to assume the role of a public person and leader in a community, and their appropriation of the human virtues that make them "men of communion." These same formators may, on occasion, teach the ways of human development and even offer some personal *mentoring* or, at times, *coaching*. More generally, they offer *encouragement, support, and challenge* along the formational path. These formators

---

10. Siegel, *Mindsight*, 172.

function exclusively in the external forum and are not to engage in matters that are reserved for the internal forum and the spiritual director.[11]

The PPF identifies a variety of ways the advisor accompanies a seminarian through the formation process:

- Encouragement
- Support
- Feedback
- Challenge
- Mentoring
- Coaching
- Assisting
- Observing

The PPF recognizes that there is no one way to accompany a seminarian. Every man enters seminary with his own history, his own family experience, and vocation story. Each man brings his own gifts and struggles. Each man has already been formed and deformed by his history. Each will need healing and freedom and each will need to discover new gifts as he makes his way through formation. Being able to relate in different ways to each seminarian requires insight into his experience, knowledge of his history, and an understanding of the ups and downs posed by the formation process. This places a great priority on the experience of the seminarian. At the same time, being able to adjust to the needs of the seminarian requires great personal freedom

---

11. *The Program of Priestly Formation*, 80, emphasis added.

and flexibility on the part of the formator. Formation does not involve shaping a man into one particular image of priesthood. It is always a matter of cooperating with what the Lord wants to do with and for this man. Besides insight and freedom, the advisor must be able to discern which approach fits with each particular seminarian. Thankfully, this complex and holy art is practiced within the context of a wise and supportive formation faculty.

Rather than describe each of the approaches to formation mentioned by the PPF, I want to highlight four fundamental skills every advisor must employ: listening, questioning, observing, and offering feedback.

Listening

Listening to another is such a rare gift in our busy world. When someone listens and is interested, the other person feels known and understood. People open up when they know they are really being listened to; they feel safe and secure; trust grows, and they share more. This is why listening is so important for formation advising. It is a skill that can be learned and developed. Most people do not listen very deeply. They are not focused on the other person, but on how they are feeling or what they will say next, or how they can solve the problem.

The first skill a formation advisor needs to develop is the skill of active listening. This kind of listening begins with awareness and attentiveness to the many ways another person expresses himself or herself. A good listener is aware of body language, the modulation of the voice, facial expressions, the pace of delivery, and the overall mood the person is in, as well as changes in mood as the conversation proceeds. An active listener seeks to understand what he has heard and what is being communicated. This means interpreting the feelings behind the words and gestures and the meaning of the words used in the conversation. A good listener must also decide how to respond to what he has received. Perhaps he will keep listening or ask a question, or offer an insight. Afterward, he responds and pays attention to the impact his response had on the person to whom he is listening.

Active listening during a formation advising meeting requires three different levels of listening.[12] The first level, known as background listening, calls for the formator to be aware of the various feelings, thoughts, and judgments that come to mind during the formation meeting. While the formator is aware of these feelings and thoughts, he keeps them in the background so he can focus on the seminarian. In the second level, the formator is focused on the seminarian: his words, expressions, what he says and does not say. A formator listens for what makes the seminarian come alive and what makes him nervous or withdrawn. This kind of listening is done in a spirit of care, interest, and compassion. The third level of listening involves reading the mood in the room. Is there energy and connection or awkwardness or a lack of energy? This information allows the formator to adjust his approach to accompanying him.

---

12. Much of this material I borrowed from Henry Kimsey-House, et al, *Co-Active Coaching: Changing Business, Transforming Lives* (Nicholas Brearly Publishing, 2011), 32–44.

Besides listening on these three levels, active listening involves the following three common practices. The first, is to articulate what is going on in the conversation. A formator can let the seminarian know what he is hearing or noticing during the formation meeting or at other times in the seminary. It can mean connecting the dots between his current experience and previous ones. It is often helpful to ask permission to share an observation, or an insight into what he is hearing or noticing. This will help the seminarian be more receptive to the observation. The second is to clarify what the formator believes he is hearing and experiencing during the conversation. This practice allows the formator to test what he is hearing and to see if he is on target while communicating to the seminarian that he is understood by the formator. It also allows the seminarian to participate in the conversation by either clarifying something or acknowledging the formator is on target. The third practice is for the formator to acknowledge, at certain times, the ways in which he sees the seminarian growing and developing in any of the dimensions of formation. This can be the recognition of emerging pastoral skills, character development such a patience, compassion, confidence, or insights into himself and others.[13]

Asking

Besides listening, formation advising depends on the art of asking good questions that move the conversation forward into deeper, more interesting, and important territory. These are open-ended questions that promote personal

---
13. *Co-Active Coaching*, 40–44.

reflection and exploration by turning a seminarian back to his experience. They explore a seminarian's desires, how he perceives the world, himself, God, the Church, and what gives him meaning. They will reveal where and how he has been formed by our consumer culture and by the gospel.[14]

The questions a formators asks a seminarian should be motivated by curiosity and a genuine interest in the person. (If a spirit of care and concern for the seminarian is the primary attitude needed for formation advising, a desire to discover who the person in front of you is runs a close second) These kinds of questions emerge out of the realization that every seminarian is a mystery to the formator and to himself. When a formator is curious, he is no longer the expert with all the answers. He does not have an agenda but desires to know and understand the person in front of him. This is quite different from an interrogation mindset that generates defensiveness. A curious mindset creates an openness and an atmosphere of mutual exploration and reflection where the seminarian finds meaning in discovering things about himself. When a formator starts with the expression "I am curious…" this gives the seminarian a chance to reflect and explore rather than be put on the spot.[15] This kind of questioning allows a formator to learn about the seminarian and understand his history, values, and motives. It is even more important for the seminarian's growth and development. Asking deep, powerful questions sends the seminarian in a direction filled with possible discoveries and mystery. It invites reflection and exploration where he

---

14. *Co-Active Coaching*, 64–65.
15. *Co-Active Coaching*, 65–68.

can learn about himself, his motives, desires and sources of meaning. This kind of learning lasts because it changes his perception of himself and others leading to real change and growth[16]

The most powerful questions are often simple, direct, and brief. Here are some examples:

- What do you want? What are you hoping for this semester?
- What was that like? Tell me more.
- What were you telling yourself as you had that experience? (This is a question about internal self-talk that can be very revelatory!)
- What about that is important to you?
- What else? What did you learn?
- What does that mean for you?
- What has been your experience of that?

These kinds of questions can help a person notice and give expression to his experience. They can lead to wonderful discussion about his relationships past and present. They will give him a chance to express his feelings, desires, memories, images, and insights. The following areas deserve special attention:

- Family experience
- Moments of transition, struggle, and conversion
- Pastoral ministry experiences
- Vocational discernment

---
16. *Co-Active Coaching*, 69–70.

Two final considerations must be kept in mind. First, some seminarians are not used to sharing their experience with others. They may have grown up in homes where no one asked them how they felt or what they think about something. It is rare for young men to have male friends with whom they can confide how they are feeling so this can be a very new experience for them. These men need to be given permission to speak about their experience. They often need language that is far more concrete than the philosophical and theological terms they learn in class.

Secondly, there are some seminarians who have a great deal to say when they come to a formation advising meeting. A formator must be aware of the extrovert who shares his thoughts, insights and opinions, but rarely speaks about his experience. With these men, it is important to direct them back to their experience by asking open-ended questions. For instance, a man may have thoughts and opinions about priesthood, celibacy, or the liturgy. Asking him about his experience of priesthood, celibacy, or liturgy opens up a very different discussion. Getting him to speak about why he wants to be a priest or what has been a meaningful experience of liturgy gets him in touch with a deeper and often different side of himself.

Observations and Feedback

Formation advisors can support and promote a seminarian's development by offering him occasional observations and feedback from the faculty. These should be communicated in the spirit of care and concern that we discussed above. The goal is for the seminarian to hear them and not act defensively so he can take them to heart and, if necessary, act on them. In our age, where communication often happens online, face-to-face communication is still the best way to share observations and offer feedback. This allows the seminarian to receive the full meaning of what you are sharing with him through your voice tone and body language. It also allows you to read how the seminarian receives and responds to your observations and feedback.

A formator regularly shares his observations with the seminarian during the formation advising meeting. For instance, a formator may note, "You seem under a lot of stress today. How are you handling that?" "You came to our meeting in a restless mood, but seem at peace now." "This was a powerful meeting. You touched on some important issues today." At different times throughout the year, it is appropriate for a formator to share observations of the seminarian's growth, where he needs to grow, and what he observes in conversation with the seminarian. These observations are based on his knowledge of the seminarian in relationship to the four dimensions of seminarian formation, the rule of life, and his understanding of the values, and practices essential for priesthood. A formator regularly observes the following features of the seminarian's life:

- Presence and participation in the common prayer and liturgical life of the seminary.
- Habits of prayer, personal piety, celibate chastity, and simplicity of life.

- Personal maturity, interpersonal skills, social skills, and leadership.
- Integration of values, virtues and qualities that characterize priestly identity and ministry.
- Mature respect for the Church, the people of God, and pastoral skill development.

There are also times when a formator will share feedback from a faculty member or the faculty as a whole. Likewise, a formator may offer the seminarian feedback, positive or negative, based on actions the seminarian has taken in the seminary community. These can be appreciative, critical, or suggestions for areas of growth. Once again, this feedback should be offered in a spirit of charity and care with the desire that the seminarian grow and learn from them.

Take Notes!

When formation advising is marked by a posture of care and the practices discussed above are employed by a formator, seminarians will share a great deal with a formator. It is important for a formator to take notes after each meeting so he can record what happened during the meeting and what he learned. At the beginning of the academic year, a formator will create a folder on each man assigned to him for formation advising. This folder contains a file with any current ministry and preaching evaluations, and the man's spring semester evaluation. It should also contain a file of notes and observations from each advising meeting. These notes are often a few lines summarizing issues and topics discussed and any observations about how the man is doing or where there is growth or insight emerging.

This can seem like a burdensome task, but it is a valuable practice for two reasons. First, it helps capture what was important about the meeting. Reviewing these notes before the next meeting will help a formator remember what was discussed in the previous meeting, and it will help him identify patterns and developments in the seminarian's formation. Secondly, when it comes to writing the evaluation, these notes become a very important resource. Without them it is impossible to recall what was discussed throughout the year during those many advising meetings! These notes will help a formator understand what happened in formation advising that year and where and how the man has grown and where he needs to grow.

Intercultural Communication

In chapter one, I discussed the multicultural contexts within which formation occurs. It was noted that many dioceses, many parishes and seminaries are multicultural environments. This can even be true of the formation advising relationship where the culture of the formator and the culture of the seminarian differ. Sociologists speak of low context and high context cultures. This distinction can help formators understand better his approach to formation advising and that of the seminarian.

In general, people from the United States tend to operate from a low context perspective while many people from countries in other parts of the world tend to operate from

Low Context	High Context
Individual-Oriented	Group-Oriented
Relies on facts	Relies on shared context
Conflicts with individuals	Conflicts with the community
Focus on facts	Focus on face saving
Focus on solutions	Focus on relationships

Actions

Direct action	Indirect response to conflict
Adjust quickly to new situations	Slow adjustment to new situations

a high context perspective. A low context person privileges individual experiences while a high context person places priority on the group, family, community, or village. Conflict and time are often approached differently. A low context person treats a conflict as a one-on-one experience. He wants to find out the facts and come to a direct solution. A high context person interprets conflict in terms of the various social relations that are impacted by the conflict. He tends to use an indirect approach to restoring relationships rather than a direct one. When it comes to new situations, such as transitioning into a seminary, a low context person adjusts quickly while a high context person takes his time adjusting because he is learning about the social environment and values building new relationships.

A formator must discover which of these two cultures the seminarian comes from. He must also learn which culture each of the men he works with comes from. For instance, a low context person appreciates direct feedback whereas a high context person will value a more indirect approach to feedback. By understanding which cultural context formed a man, a formator will better understand how that seminarian will adapt to the culture of the seminary. When a formator works with someone from a different cultural context or when the seminarian finds his culture differs from the seminary, he needs to draw on two skills. First, he must come to understand and appreciate the culture the man comes from. One is not better than another. Secondly, the formator must act as a bridge builder either between himself and the seminarian or the seminarian and the seminary culture. This requires discernment. There will be times when a low context approach to formation advising is warranted and there will be times when a high context approach is called for.

Accompanying Seminarians throughout the Year

As I discussed above, formation advising is the practice of attentively accompanying a seminarian as he engages the formation process. A formator must be attentive to the two ways every seminarian experiences the formation process. On the one hand, each seminarian's experience is shaped by the schedule of the academic year. At the same time, each man is at a particular stage in the formation process. A formator must be attentive to the academic calendar and where a seminarian is within the formation process. Being aware of the two different dimensions of the seminary experience informs how the advisor accompanies a seminarian.

For instance, a fourth-year theologian who is about to be ordained to the priesthood faces issues that are quite different from a pre-theologian just out of college during his first semester in seminary. What a seminarian is experiencing as he returns to seminary after a summer assignment is quite different from how he feels during midterms.

The following calendar identifies common themes to discuss with seminarians during the year. It also lists topics to discuss based on the year in formation.

Discussions at the Beginning of the Year

Set up meetings with advisees. Google calendar is helpful. It is best to meet on the week he is not meeting his spiritual director.

- Each seminary determines how often advisors meet with seminarians. The *Ratio* calls for regular meetings with advisees.
- Most formation faculty meet weekly.
  - New Men
    - Discuss summer experience
    - Learn about family life, (particularly what were the joys and struggles of growing up in his family) and life history
    - Learn about vocation story, ask how family responded to his vocation
    - Review file of new advisees
    - Pay attention to their transition experience during the first few months
  - Returning Men

- Review summer experience
- Review Pastoral Year (pay attention to their transition)
  - All Men
    - Hand out and describe the formation goal setting process
    - Discuss what they have written regarding goals

Discussions in the Spring Semester

- Early in January, review their retreat experience
  - Discuss the community workshop
  - Discuss ministry selection for next fall

Discussions throughout the Year

- All New Seminarians
  - Discuss transition
  - Discuss assumptions, expectations, stress
- First Theology
  - Discuss vocational discernment
  - Discuss ministry (catechesis or RCIA)
- Second Theology
  - Discuss Hospital Ministry and Basic Supervised Ministry
  - Discuss small group experience and celibacy
- Third Theology
  - For those returning from a pastoral year, discuss their experience.
  - Discuss preaching classes, especially the evaluations seminarians receive from their professors.

- Discuss their particular parish ministry
- Discuss shadowing experiences with pastor
- Discuss diaconate promises
- Discuss his desire to be ordained to the priesthood including his desire to preach God's Word, offer the sacraments and lead God's people.
- Fourth Theology
  - Discuss transition out of seminary
  - Discuss how his experience as a deacon has confirmed his desire to be a priest
  - Discuss preaching in the parish
  - Discuss any sacramental experiences
  - Read and discuss Michael White's *Rebuilt: Awakening the Faithful, Reaching the Lost, and Making Church Matter* and Fr. James Mallon's *Divine Renovation*.

Formation Issues throughout the Four Years of Formation

As a seminarian progresses through the four years of formation for the priesthood, there are certain events and issues related to the four dimensions of formation that a formator should discuss with a seminarian. It is not easy to keep these various events and issues in mind as a formator meets with one seminarian after another with each man at a different stage in the formation process. What follows is a listing of key issues to be discussed with advisees according to each of the four dimensions of formation for each of the four years of formation. The list is not exhaustive but offers the advisor a quick glance at the issues he needs to discuss with his advisee at some point during the year. The next chapter fleshes out more fully how a formation advisor approaches and handles each dimension of formation.[17]

Human Formation

First Year
- Adjustment to the life and routine of the seminary
- Family of origins, life story and vocation story
- Previous seminary experience
- Trust and openness to the formation process
- Growing self-awareness
- Clear awareness of sexual orientation
- Growth in self-discipline and prudence
- Participating in the life of the community

Second Year
- Ability to manage and/or abstain from addictive substances and addictive behaviors
- Adjusting to clerical life
- Aware of emotional issues that shape his life
- Developing friendships
- Awareness of celibacy as more than genital deprivation
- Developing the habit of self-care:
  - Healthy bedtime habits: what is your bedtime routine?
  - Exercises: What do you do for exercise?
  - Nutrition: What are you eating and when are you eating?

---

17. Father Melvin Blanchette, PSS, "Negotiating the Pillars of Formation" (Unpublished) offers a year-by-year list of the various issues to be discussed by formators with seminarians based on the four pillars in his article "Negotiating the Pillars of Formation." This section of the handbook is indebted to Father Blanchett's article.

- Identifying and growing free from perfectionist tendencies
- Feelings regarding hospital ministry

Third Year
- Discuss the pastoral year experience with all returning from that experience
- Resolution of major therapeutic needs
- Peaceful acceptance of sexual orientation and needs
- Comfortable with solitude
- Accepting of his talents, weaknesses and limits
- Understands the need for exercise and good health
- Growing ability to recognize and understand the emotions of others
- Learning how to handle relationships with friends, family and parishioners
- Emerging spirit of generosity

Fourth Year
- Ability to make sound decisions
- Transitioning out of seminary into full-time priestly ministry
- Awareness of celibacy as a gift
- Ability to remain part of the life in the house while preparing to move on
- Ability to listen to others without judgment
- Discuss approaches to leadership and conflict
- Anticipating emotional support systems after ordination

Spiritual Formation

First Year
- Developing the habit of reflecting on his experience and understanding the value of this practice.
- Discuss the relationship between actions and their moral and spiritual consequences
- Discuss his prayer practices and participation in the communal liturgy.
- Demonstrates insight into God calling him to seminary.

Second Year
- Role of Scripture in prayer
- Discuss adjustment to the clerical life
- Discuss his understanding and experience of celibacy
- Growing simplicity of life
- Developing a spirit of generosity in the house and in ministry
- Growing free from perfectionism

Third Year
- Clarity and commitment to his vocation
- Readiness to pray the Liturgy of the Hours
- Increased integration of spiritual and pastoral life
- Realistic acknowledgement of evil balanced with hope
- Emerging spirit of compassion and mercy

Fourth Year
- Ongoing commitment to spiritual and intellectual formation

- How has diaconate prepared him for priesthood?
- Ability to see celibacy as a gift
- Integrate obedience and holiness
- Ability to listen to others
- Emerging identity as a leader of the faith community

Intellectual Formation

First Year
- Discuss study habits and adjustment to graduate work in theology
- Impact of social media on study habits
- Developing historical consciousness
- A growing appreciation for the human and divine in the church
- Receptive to the ideas and experiences of others

Second Year
- Developing a realistic understanding of the church as human and divine
- Making connections between theology and ministry

Third Year
- Connections between Scripture, theology and preaching
- Able to integrate theological concepts into life experience

Fourth Year
- Discussions about ecclesiology and parish life

Pastoral Formation

First Year
- Discuss previous ministry experience
- Selecting ministry with the poor
- Reflection on their ministry experience

Second Year
- Hospital Ministry
  - Reflections on case studies
  - Reviewing verbatims from hospital ministry
  - Reflection on experience with an eye to human formation issues and pastoral skill development

Third Theology
- Preaching I and II
  - Discuss the experience of preaching
  - Discuss how he prepares his homilies
  - Discuss his struggles and areas of growth
  - Review preaching evaluations
- Parish Ministry I
  - Discuss parish ministry experience of the people, staff and pastor.

Fourth Theology
- Parish Ministry II
  - Discuss preaching and sacramental practice in the parish.
  - Discuss *Rebuilt* and *Great Catholic Parishes*

3 | Formation Advising and the Gift of Accompaniment

IN THE PREVIOUS CHAPTER, I presented a general introduction to the work of formation advising with an emphasis on accompaniment marked by care and concern for the seminarian as he engages each dimension of formation. I described the basic skills a formator must develop to accompanying a seminarian through the formation process. The present chapter goes into detail about how to accompany a seminarian through the different dimensions of formation. I begin with a suggestion of how to introduce a seminarian to formation advising. Then I identify the levels of listening a formator engages in as he accompanies a seminarian throughout formation advising. These begin with getting to know a seminarian, accompanying him through human formation issues, listening for his vocational discernment, and helping him with his pastoral skill development in the process of becoming a disciple and conforming to Christ the Shepherd and Servant.

Introducing a Seminarian to Formation Advising

When meeting with a new seminarian for the first time, it is helpful to explain to him your understanding of and approach to formation advising. Often seminarians come to formation advising feeling nervous and unsure about the purpose and process. By explaining your role as a formation advisor, the purpose of formation advising, and how you expect the seminarian to participate in advising, you will alleviate some of his anxiety and help create some initial rapport with him.

Begin by sharing with him the conviction that the Lord is the formator. This sets the entire formation advising process in a spiritual framework that resonates with seminarians. The seminary is a school of the Gospel where each seminarian is led in his formation by Christ. The Lord will use every dimension of seminary life to form this man into the person and priest Christ is calling him to become. As the formator, Christ acts like a potter who seeks to shape, trim, and mold each seminarian into his image. Formation, therefore, takes on a cruciform shape as the seminarian is asked to rid himself of all that is opposed to the Gospel, while the Holy Spirit cultivates in him healthy and holy habits and skills. When formation is understood in this way, cooperation becomes crucial. Faculty and seminarians must cooperate with the many ways the Lord seeks to form a man into his image.

Next, spend some time explaining your role as a formation advisor. Discuss how a formator accompanies and guides a seminarian through the formation process. Let him know how important it is that you get to know him—his life story, vocation story, and current experiences—so he can come to know himself and you can help him discern the ways Christ is calling him to grow and change. This will also help you represent him to the formation faculty as well as provide a larger context for understanding whatever formation issues come up. Explain how, throughout the academic year, a formator listens to the seminarian, offers him feedback, and in the spring semester, writes an evaluation that summarizes where and how the man has grown and where he needs to grow.

Formation advising meetings can be a real mystery to seminarians. It is important to stress that these are conversations, not advice sessions or counseling sessions. These conversations are structured around the experience of the seminarian and the formator's effort to understand the seminarian's current experience in the light of the various dimensions of formation. As a formator listens, he may ask questions and offer observations to gain further insight into the seminarian's experience. This, in turn, will allow the formator to help the seminarian grow in self-knowledge.

Formation advising meetings take on real depth and meaning when the seminarian spends time preparing for these meetings. I encourage seminarians who see me for formation advising to spend time in prayer reflecting over the events of the past two weeks. I ask them to recall the key events, what they meant to them, how they felt at the time, and where God was found in those events. I also ask seminarians to notice any connections between what happened in the past two weeks and where they are growing and need to grow. This practice must be scheduled into their calendar. Since Christ is the formator, active participation by a seminarian in the formation process is a crucial way he can cooperate with the Lord. This kind of work transforms formation advising meetings from a report of activities to a meaningful discussion about what is happening in his life. Furthermore, this kind of reflection puts the seminarian in touch with the deeper dimensions of his experience where the real work of formation happens.

Levels of Listening

In the previous chapter, I discussed the practice of listening as an essential skill that a formator must develop in order to accompanying a seminarian through the formation process. Here, I expand on the skill of listening by identifying four levels of listening and observation formation advisors need to develop in formation advising. Each level is deeper than the previous one.

- First, formators need to listen to and understand the seminarian's past and present experience as he engages in all four dimensions of the formation process. This includes learning what gifts and potential he brings to the seminary.
- Second, by getting to know a seminarian's story, the formator can begin to listen for the deeper human formation issues that are unique to him. This will involve noticing when these issues emerge, offering him support, insight, and occasional feedback.
- Third, the formator listens on the level of spiritual formation. This includes listening for the role God plays

in a seminarian's vocation, his relationships, and ministry, and the images of God, Christ, and the Church the seminarian carries with him. At the same time the formator is listening for growing clarity regarding the man's vocation.
- Fourth, the formator listens to a seminarian's experience of ministry and the seminarian's response to his ministry courses to discern the emergence of pastoral skills and the attitude of a generous servant.

As a formator listens to a seminarian in the four ways described above, he will notice where the seminarian needs to grow and where and when growth is occurring. Helping a seminarian discover and grow free from whatever prevents him from becoming a disciple and an image of Christ the Good Shepherd and Servant is essential to formation advising. As a formator gets to know a seminarian, he must ask himself, "Are there parts of this man's experience that can prevent him from relating to others in a mature way, from becoming a disciple, and cooperating with Christ as a priest? What attitudes, assumptions, and behaviors does this man need to let go of?" These questions point to the need for an emphasis on human formation and attention to his family of origin. They will also reveal where the man needs healing, support, and perhaps even counseling. At the same time, a formator needs to notice, affirm, and support a man's growth especially in human and pastoral formation. He must look for where and when a seminarian is embracing the vision of the kingdom of God. The formator must support and promote the emergence of dispositions, virtues, and skills that reflect the Gospel. This is what makes formation advising a dynamic and exciting ministry. Most seminary formation programs offer key moments when these obstacles emerge and when growth occurs such as the transition into seminary, ministry with the poor, hospital ministry, preaching courses, a pastoral year, and third- and fourth-year parish ministry experiences.

Accompaniment: Getting to Know a Seminarian

Accompanying a seminarian through the formation process means getting to know him by learning his life story and his vocation story.[1] A formator can learn a great deal about a person by listening to him recount his experience of his family of origin, what it was like to grow up in his family, who were his friends, and what high school and college were like. By understanding this story, a formator will have a better sense of the experiences, desires, gifts, and struggles a man brings to seminary.

The following questions can help a formator learn about the family of origin:

- How would you describe your parents' relationship? How did you get along with your brothers and sisters?
- What were the rules, values, and beliefs in your family that most shape who you are?

---

[1]. *Ratio*, "It is important for every seminarian to be aware of his own life history, and be ready to share it with his formators. This would include especially his experience of childhood and adolescence, the influence his family and relatives have exercised upon him, his ability to establish mature and well-balanced interpersonal relationships, or his lack thereof, and his ability to handle positively moments of solitude," 94.

- What were the unwritten rules in your family of origin?
- Who was the person closest to you growing up?
- What topics of conversation, feelings, behaviors, and thoughts were forbidden in your family?
- Do you see how your early family life influences your current relationship with others? What are positive influences? What are the difficult parts?

After learning about his family of origin, a formator will benefit from learning about a seminarian's high school and college experiences. Who were his friends? What were his favorite activities? Did he work or take on leadership positions? Understanding his previous seminary experience and ministry experience fills out this picture. Reviewing the application and reading the autobiography of a man a formator works with is also very valuable.

Listening to a man review his life story allows a formator to have some insight into the people and events that have formed him up to this moment. This practice helps the seminarian to develop a consistent narrative identity. Knowing his past can help him make sense of his present life. It can help him to grow free from unexamined elements of his past that often determine his decisions and reactions in the present.

Transitions

Another important time for formators to learn about a seminarian's experience is during the many and varied transitions that make up seminary life. There is the transition into seminary and the transition into full-time priesthood.

Every year, seminarians transition back into the seminary after the summer and after winter break. Each of these transition moments affords the formator an opportunity to learn more about the people he works with and to help the seminarian learn about himself. The approach a formator takes to accompany a person through any of these transitions must be marked by care for the man and curiosity about his experience. For the man first entering seminary, everything is new. He is often filled with worries and expectations. Offering him a chance to express what he is experiencing is very important to a successful transition. A formator will regularly check in with the seminarian about his transition, how he feels about being in seminary and in school again, and how is he adjusting to the daily schedule, getting to class, beginning to study, and making friends in the house. With returning seminarians, it is important to discuss their summer experience including time with family and their experience of ministry during the summer. It is also important to find out how he feels about returning to seminary.

Accompanying a person through these different transition periods is an important part of the formator's role in the formation process. Formation advising can be a safe nonjudgmental space where the seminarian can express how he is feeling about his transition. It gives him a chance to make sense of what he is experiencing and can be an opportunity for the formator to suggest ways to handle the transition.

For many men, the most difficult transition they go through is returning to seminary from pastoral year. A formator can be a source of comfort and understanding for men as they go through this process. These men have left full-time parish ministry to return to studies. The makeup of the house is often very different from the one they left when they went on pastoral year. It is important to review with the seminarian his pastoral year taking into account the four dimensions of formation. It is also important to attend to his adjustment to seminary life. The following questions can guide a formator's conversations with a man returning from pastoral year:

1. How did you adjust to rectory living and parish life?
2. How well did you integrate yourself into the staff and lay volunteers in the parish? Where did you have to adjust your expectations, attitude, and approach?
3. What skills and gifts for ministry did you discover during your pastoral year?
4. What personal limits or weaknesses did you discover about yourself? How well were you able to accept them? How are you handling them?
5. In the midst of a busy pastoral year, how well did you care for yourself through exercise, diet, and a balanced lifestyle?
6. How well did you use the gifts God gave you during pastoral year? Specifically, how punctual and responsive were you in various pastoral situations?
7. What prayer practices did you maintain during pastoral year? Did you adopt any new ones?
8. What opportunities did you have during pastoral year to interpret what you have learned in your studies to help the people make sense of their experience of life

and God? How did the people respond to your preaching, presentations, and conversations? How well did you use language people could understand and relate to in your conversations and preaching?
9. How would you describe your presence in public liturgies? Were there times when you were faithful, sincere, and engaging or mechanical and detached?
10. Did your pastoral experience help you understand the relationship between spirituality and pastoral practice? Have you had to adjust your expectations?
11. What impact did your pastoral year have on your own vocational discernment?

Understanding His Daily Experience of Formation

Each time a formator meets with a seminarian, he tries to understand what has been the man's experience since they last met, and what is most on his mind and heart. This is where our discussion of curiosity, care, and open-ended questions becomes important. There will be a discussion of tasks he has to complete—papers, reading, ministry—but at some point the discussion should explore different dimensions of a man's experience depending on the topic. It is always safe to assume there are multiple levels to a person's experience and it can take a while for a person to understand what those are and begin to share that insight. Not every event or topic requires a deep exploration, but a skilled formator learns when something of importance comes up and is worth exploring.

At the conclusion of the previous chapter, I listed events that occur during the academic year and at important moments in the formation process that formators regularly speak about to advisees. A topic of regular conversation will be a seminarian's experience with his family, with men in the house, and with people in ministry. A formator will be aware of how a seminarian is handling classes, what his attitude toward studies is, what his study habits are, and how is he feeling about midterms or finals. He will know about the man's relationships and activities in the house. A seminarian's experience of ministry will be a regular topic of discussion, especially challenging ones like ministry with the poor and hospital ministry. Likewise, formators will know about a man's spiritual practices and where he is with his discernment of his priestly vocation and call to chaste celibacy. He can learn a great deal by discussing the main takeaways from the man's annual retreat. For seminarians in third and fourth theology, formators will discuss the experience of preparing for preaching and the act of preaching in class and, once ordained, at Mass. A more complete list of topics to discuss in formation advising can be found in the previous chapter.

Intercultural Communication

As I mentioned in chapter one, formation today happens within a multicultural context.[2] A seminarian will need to learn about and negotiate the cultures within his diocese, within the seminary, and in his ministry assignment. The encounter and clash between cultures in each of these settings needs to be navigated by the seminarian. The chart

---

2. This material is based on a lecture given by Dr. Arturo Chavez at Theological College on January 25 and 26, 2018.

Low Context	*High Context*
Individual-Oriented	Group-Oriented
Relies on facts	Relies on shared context
Conflicts with individuals	Conflicts with the community
Focus on facts	Focus on face saving
Focus on solutions	Focus on relationships

Actions

Direct action	Indirect response to conflict
Adjust quickly to new situations	Slow adjustment to new situations

above is a reminder of the differences between low and high context cultures.

Formation advising can be a helpful place where a seminarian can make sense of his encounter with these various cultures. As a formator gets to know whether the seminarian comes from a low or high context culture, he will be able to help him understand and navigate the complexities of the seminary culture and the culture of his diocese. Understanding the different approaches to relationships, time, and conflict taken by a low- and high-context culture can help a formator understand a seminarian's experience of seminary and ministry. At the same time, a formator can transform a seminarian's experience of seminary and ministry by teaching him about the differences between a low and high context culture. It can be very eye opening for a seminarian to learn which culture formed him. It is also important that he grow to understand neither culture is better than the other. They are just different and need to be appreciated as such.

Accompaniment: Understanding His Vocation Story and His Call to Chaste Celibacy

I have been stressing how accompanying a seminarian through the formation process involves getting to know his life story and how he handles transitions and current seminary experiences. He will also learn about his vocation story and how he understands and responds to the Church's call to chaste celibacy. By asking a seminarian to prayerfully review and tell his vocation story, he can discover some of the depth and mystery involved in that experience and the ways God was involved in it.

As a formator listens to a man's vocation story, he will keep the following questions in mind:

- When did you first consider becoming a priest?
- When and how did that thought or desire begin to emerge for you?
- How did you react to this at first?
- What experiences led you to decide to enter seminary?
- How did your family and friends react to this?
- Why are you choosing the diocesan priesthood?
- Where are you now with discernment regarding priesthood?

While discernment can be an internal forum matter, a formation advisor needs to know where a man stands regarding his vocation. Most men gradually gain clarity about their vocation during first and second theology. Formators check in at least twice a year with a seminarian regarding his discernment, once at the beginning of the fall semester and after the annual retreat.

The practice of checking in with a man on his vocational discernment includes his sense of God's call to diocesan priesthood, how he feels about the call, and how he feels about living a chaste celibate life. There are times when a man discerns a call to religious life or discerns that God is not calling him to ordained priesthood. A skilled formator can help a man with this discernment by sharing with him two approaches to discerning God's will suggested by St. Ignatius of Loyola and described in Father Timothy Gallagher's book *Discerning the Will of God: An Ignatian Guide to Christian Decision Making*.[3]

Listening to a seminarian's vocation story, a formator will also inquire about the seminarian's call to chaste celibacy. Although celibacy is a topic regularly discussed in spiritual direction, formation advisors will also need to discuss various dimensions of the commitment to chaste celibacy with their advisees as part of the practice of accompanying them through seminary. These discussions are meant to help a seminarian discern his call to chaste celibacy, understand what it means, and learn how he is to live out this commitment. Celibacy is a complex topic. Formators can approach the many dimensions of celibacy by keeping in mind the four dimensions of formation. Every seminarian's experience and understanding of celibacy

---

3. Timothy Gallagher, *Discerning the Will of God: An Ignatian Guide to Christian Decision Making* (New York: Crossroads Publishing Company, 2009).

will be shaped by the current cultural attitudes towards celibacy. As a formator listens to a seminarian describe his experience and understanding of celibacy, he will keep in mind this cultural context. This is the approach taken by Paul VI in *Sacerdotalis Caelibatus* and the Sulpician Father's document on formation for celibacy, *For the Sake of the Kingdom*.[4] Both documents reflected on the positive and negative cultural attitudes regarding celibacy. For instance, young people today value authenticity, generosity, and giving of oneself. At the same time, we live in a highly "sexualized" consumer culture that struggles with commitment, dismisses the Church as irrelevant, and often considers celibacy as unnatural and even strange. It will be important to discuss these cultural attitudes, to what extent he has been influenced by them, and discover how he feels about living a chaste celibate life.

As a man proceeds through the early stages of formation, it will be important to discuss with him his understanding of celibacy. He should be familiar with the magisterial documents and the biblical foundations of celibacy as he develops his own positive understanding of this charism.[5] Paul VI's encyclical and the Sulpician document locate celibacy within the context of the kingdom of God, Christ's devotion to the kingdom, and the life of the Church. Set within this context, celibacy is a particular form of discipleship that imitates Christ's gift of self to the kingdom. This imitation of Christ manifests itself as the total self-gift of the celibate

---

4. Paul VI, Encyclical Letter *Sacerdotalis Caelibatus* (June 24, 1967). Accessed at http://www.vatican.va/content/paul-vi/en/encyclicals.index.html. *For the Sake of the Kingdom* (Paris: Society of the Priests of St. Sulpice, 2005).

5. One study is done by Fr. Ronald Witherup PSS, The *Seminary Journal* 9, no. 2, (Fall 2003).

to Christ and in service to God's people so that they will grow into the new humanity made possible by Jesus' death and resurrection.[6] Celibacy, then, is a unique way of relating to Christ and the people of God. Such a Christ-centered, kingdom-focused act of self-gift and self-service will help a seminarian to connect celibacy to human formation, his spiritual life, and his pastoral formation.

Since celibacy is, by its very nature, relational, human formation plays an important role in the development of a healthy and holy celibate life.[7] This cannot be stated enough. The celibate's renunciation of marriage fosters in him the capacity to open himself to others in a unique way. Consequently, all the work that goes into human formation impacts celibacy. This includes emotional intelligence, the capacity to relate to others, the ability to listen, and the cultivation of virtues such as self-denial, humility, responsibility, hospitality, prudence, and availability, among others.[8]

Formators will also need to discuss the sacrifices and struggles that come with celibacy and the importance of self-care.[9] There are the obvious sacrifices of an exclusive inti-

---

6. On the relationship between the kingdom of God and imitating Christ's self-gift also see Howard P. Bleichner, PSS, and Daniel M. Buechlein, OSB, and Robert F. Leavitt, PSS, *Celibacy for the Kingdom: Theological Reflections and Practical Perspectives* (Baltimore: St. Mary's 1990, reprinted by Criterion Press, 1997).

7. This is a major theme in the Sulpician document on celibacy. See, 11, 14–15, 18–19.

8. The cultivation of virtues necessary for relating to others as a celibate is discussed by Paul VI, 70, John Paul II in *Pastores Dabo Vobis*, 43, and the Sulpician document on page 18.

9. The following material is based on a lecture by psychologist Kathy Galleher, Ph.D, given at Theological College in Washington, DC, in the spring of 2019.

mate partner, marriage, sex, children, and family life. When men begin attending the weddings of their friends, this sacrifice can become clearer to them. These are moments when formators can engage in this discussion. There is also the loneliness that comes with celibacy and the stress of nonstop parish ministry. Under the theme of self-knowledge, formators will discuss with seminarians how they handle stress, pain, and loneliness. What are positive and restorative practices and what are less helpful practices? It will be important for men to learn the signs of when they are getting depleted of energy and the meaning that gives life to ministry. Drinking, overeating, pornography, and overspending are common and addictive ways people cope with stress and loneliness. Then there is "junk food for the soul" such as surfing the web, endless TV watching, and superficial conversations that turn into venting sessions. Formators will help men identify harmful ways of coping that need to be replaced with healthy ways of handling stress. Seminary is a time for a man to develop physical, emotional, social, spiritual, and intellectual habits that will help him cope with life's struggles. For diocesan priests, this will always include developing and maintaining relationships with family and friends, fellow priests, and the people in the parish.

Spiritual formation is fundamental to living a chaste celibate life. It is important that a formator check in with his advisee twice a year about his discernment regarding chaste celibacy. Celibacy is born out of a desire to grow in union with Christ and to abandon oneself to Christ and his kingdom. It is a choice made in an effort to grow closer to Christ and to imitate his self-giving life for the sake of the kingdom of God. As Father George Aschenbrenner, SJ, suggests, celibacy is a response to Christ's call and to Christ's love. The spiritual life of the celibate must be rooted in the attractiveness of God's love. Furthermore, it must be fed by a threefold relationship: with Christ, with fellow priests, and with the people in the parish and in ministry for the people of God.[10] As a formator checks in with a man about his understanding of celibacy, he will also discuss with him the relationship between celibacy and his spiritual life. Part of that discussion will include distorted ways to live the celibate life, such as the bachelor syndrome, workaholism, clericalism, and private individualism. Following this discussion will be conversations about spiritual practices that can feed and sustain the celibate. These will include spiritual direction; personal prayer, especially the examen and *lectio*; retreats; the cultivation of virtues; and friendships. It will also be important to help a seminarian distinguish between loneliness and solitude. He will face times of loneliness but it is his solitude that can create a space for hearing God's Word and receiving God's love that can be shared with the people in powerful ways. This is something he will have to discover for himself as he lives the celibate life.

Perhaps the sign that formation for celibacy has taken hold is the emergence in a seminarian of pastoral charity. "The whole formation imparted to candidates for the priesthood aims at preparing them to enter into communion with the charity of Christ the Good Shepherd."[11] Pastoral charity

---

10. George A. Aschenbrenner, SJ, *Quickening the Fire in Our Midst: The Challenge of Diocesan Priestly Spirituality* (Chicago: Loyola Press, 2002), 110–115.

11. *Pastores Dabo Vobis*, 21.

includes the capacity to love a community and a people, an ability to show warmth and care and to be available. It will involve relating to women in a positive fashion. Contemplating how Jesus in the Gospels relates to people, especially women, can be a powerful spiritual practice that will feed his capacity to love. The other practice that will teach him to love as Jesus loves is the daily practice of gratitude. That practice will help him remember that he is loved and called to love as Christ loves.

Accompaniment: Human Formation Issues

Recent magisterial teaching maintains that human formation is the foundation for the other dimensions of formation. There are two good reasons for this emphasis on human formation. The first reason concerns the spiritual life of the priest. The Christian spiritual life is based on our relationship with Christ lived within the Christian community empowered by the Holy Spirit. That relationship grows and develops as a seminarian learns to hear and respond to the voice of Christ and the inspiration of the Holy Spirit. Unresolved human formation issues can make it difficult to hear and respond to Christ, especially when the voice of Christ and movements of the Holy Spirit are drowned by the voice of his parents, his pain, his anger, and his internal critic. Rather than responding to the call and will of Jesus, he will end up reacting to his own needs and wounds thereby undermining his ability to be a disciple of Christ and a priest.

The second reason concerns the demands of priestly ministry. It requires that a priest develop a mature capacity for relationships with men and women. It calls for leadership skills, the ability to handle conflict, and the skill to make difficult decisions while providing a vision for the parish. He is to be a servant leader modeled after Christ the Good Shepherd and Servant. Unresolved human formation issues can undermine a priest's ability to relate to others in a mature way. They can drain him of energy. These issues can prevent him from making difficult decisions, leading in a manner that promotes the Gospel, and providing and promoting a vision for the parish. Distorted assumptions and attitudes about others, especially women and minorities will also undermine a priest's ability to lead the parish community so the people come to know and serve the Gospel. The Church of the future needs priests who can walk with the people of God and lead them in a healthy and holy Christ-like manner.

When a formator spends time getting to know a seminarian, he will discover the kinds of human formation issues each man needs to address during the first few years of formation. This is the benefit of learning about a seminarian's life story, what he says about his early home life, his relationship with his parents, and his friendships. So many formation issues stem from these early life experiences. There are others that come from experiences that happened in school and through other life experiences. Often a human formation issue can take time to surface either because the seminarian is not aware of it or he is reluctant to speak about it. This is why it is so important to listen to a man's experience and explore with him his thoughts and feelings as he moves through the formation process.

Though not exhaustive, the following is a list of common issues formation advisors will hear about and discuss with seminarians:

- Difficulties associated with their family of origin
- Low self-esteem, lack of self-confidence, lack of self-acceptance
- Fears, anxieties, anger, depression
- Loneliness and unresolved grief
- Sexual orientation, not being able to accept oneself due to homosexual orientation, and lack of information and early religious formation
- Perfectionism and distorted self-images
- Addictions and trauma
- Internet pornography
- Control issues and issues with authority[12]

Most formation issues impact how a man views himself and God and how he relates to others. For this reason, a formator must help a man notice and address them. A formator needs to listen for when and where these issues surface in the seminarian's experience. He should pay attention to a seminarian's experiences in community, his relationships in the seminary, and how he handles the more intense experiences of ministry, such as ministry with the poor, hospital ministry, and preaching. These are the common situations where formation issues emerge.

It is important to remember that a formator is not an interrogator but someone who listens with the understanding

---

12. I want to thank Fr. Mel Blanchette, PSS, for his help in putting this list together.

that these issues can come up from time to time. The point is to help a seminarian notice when these issues emerge so he can address them. Formators need to gently explore these issues with advisees. This can only be done after rapport and trust have been established. Many of these issues originate in a painful situation and should be explored in a caring and gentle manner. It is important to create an environment where the seminarian feels comfortable discussing them. It is not uncommon for advisors to recommend that a seminarian seek out professional counseling to help resolve these issues. Often, real growth and insight result from working with a counselor. A formator will learn a great deal about a seminarian by discussing with him any insights he has gained and growth he has experienced by seeing a counselor.

Engaging a man's human formation issues can be challenging but it is also very rewarding work. When a seminarian engages the formation process and addresses his human formation issues, growth occurs. He gradually grows free from past wounds and distorted attitudes and behaviors. He begins to develop new Gospel-shaped attitudes and virtues and new ways of relating to other people. Formators can help a seminarian to see when and where this happens by acknowledging, affirming, and supporting this growth and development. For instance, a formator should acknowledge how the man who struggled with self-confidence in his first few years in seminary now displays confidence as a deacon serving at the liturgy. Similarly, the formator should affirm how a man who struggled with family of origin issues now reacts to situations in ways that differ from what he learned from his family. By drawing a seminarian's attention to his growing freedom and newfound attitudes and virtues, the formator reinforces this growth and encourages the man to continue in this direction.

Cultivating the Capacity for Relationships

As mentioned above, the goal of human formation is the development of a mature capacity for relations with men and women of various ages and social conditions.[13] The process of developing such a capacity is long and complex. It involves a man growing in maturity, self-knowledge, self-confidence, and inner freedom. His relationship with the men in the house, with his formator and spiritual director, and the people he encounters in ministry will be the places where this capacity to relate to others emerges. A formator can play an important role in this process by offering a seminarian feedback about the way he relates to others, and suggestions for different ways to relate to others. For those who come from homes where healthy relationships were the norm and have a secure attachment, this process began very early in life. For those who grew up in difficult home situation that did not provide a secure attachment, this process may not begin until seminary.

Developing the capacity to relate to others in a mature way depends on the development of three fundamental skills: self-awareness, self-management, and social awareness. These skills are regularly associated with emotional

---

13. *Ratio*, 95.

intelligence.[14] Formators may find themselves spending a great deal of time with certain seminarians developing these skills. Even men who come from healthy homes and have a secure attachment will need to develop some of these skills. Self-awareness refers to a person's capacity to perceive his own emotions in the moment and to understand how he tends to react emotionally in various situations over time. It requires the skill of self-management where a person uses his awareness of his emotions to be flexible in social situations by directing his behavior in ways appropriate to the current situation. This requires impulse control and the personal freedom to put his needs on hold and to be able to manage his personal tendencies to be in the service of the other. Social awareness refers to the ability to pick up on the emotions of others. The more a person is aware of his own emotions, the more he will be able to perceive what other people are thinking and feeling. This too requires the ability to recognize and modulate his emotions. Often, it means he must stop talking and stop the monologue in his head in order to listen and observe others. This skill comes into play in the dining hall, when preaching, or leading a parish meeting. Skilled preachers and leaders are experts are reading the room and adjusting to the mood of the people. A priest must learn to do the same to be successful in ministry.[15]

---

14. This material is based on the book written by Travis Bradberry and Jean Greaves, *Emotional Intelligence 2.0* (San Diego, CA: TalentSmart Publishers, 2009). I regularly read and discuss this book with first-year theologians who struggle with self-awareness, self-management, and social awareness. Many men find it very helpful. This book gives men language for emotional intelligence as well as examples and exercises for developing the relational skills associated with it.

15. Bradberry and Greaves, *Emotional Intelligence 2.0*, 32–39.

The following are strategies a formator should advise a seminarian to practice to develop the three skills of emotional intelligence.[16]

Self-Awareness
- Observe the impact of your emotions on others.
- Pay attention to emotions you seek to avoid
- Feel where in your body your emotions express themselves
- Know who and what pushes your buttons
- Keep a journal of your emotions
- Get to know yourself under stress, both what you feel and what you tell yourself

Self-Management
- Learn the power of breathing
- Count to ten
- Sleep on it
- Replace negative self-talk with positive self-talk
- Get quality sleep
- Exercise
- Expect change to come

Social Awareness
- Greet people by name
- Watch the other person's body language
- Plan ahead for social gatherings
- Learn to listen

---

16. Bradberry and Greaves, *Emotional Intelligence 2.0*. These strategies are found on pages 61–175.

- Put yourself in the other person's shoes
- Catch the mood of the room

Every priest needs to develop friendships to support his life and ministry. He also needs to be able to relate well with others to engage in priestly ministry. These features of priestly life depend on his having in place the skills of self-awareness, self-management, and social awareness. In every friendship and ministry situation, a priest must be aware of his emotions and be able to read the emotional state of those who come to him for friendship and ministry. He will be able to develop relationships by drawing on his own self-awareness and his awareness of others to communicate and bond with them. Formators can learn how well a seminarian has developed the three skills and how well he uses them in his relationship and ministry by discussing with him those friendships and ministry experiences. The following are strategies formators can recommend to seminarians for developing relationships with family, friends, and in ministry:

- Be open and curious
- Match body language and voice tone with message
- Build trust
- Little things matter
- Acknowledge the other person's emotions

Accompaniment: Priestly Ministry Skill Development

What makes seminary meaningful and enjoyable for most men is their experience of ministry and the practical and pastoral courses they take. As a man moves through the formation process, he is given a variety of ministry experiences including a ministry with the poor, parish catechesis, hospital ministry, and parish ministry during third and fourth theology. The various ministry courses, especially his preaching courses, and practicums are designed to help him develop the skills needed for priestly ministry. By listening to a man's experience in these courses and in ministry, the formator can learn how well a seminarian is learning to listen, preach, and develop leadership skills and the ability to lead the people of God through the various rites and liturgies of our faith.

These experiences and courses are exciting and challenging for most seminarians. They can be a fruitful source of discussion in formation advising. A seminarian will need a formator who can accompany him through his struggles and growth in pastoral formation by listening to him, supporting him, and encouraging him. As a man begins to develop confidence and new skills, recognition of this development by his formator or other faculty can encourage his growth. He will also benefit from feedback and suggestion from his formator as well as further reading. These experiences often reveal areas for further human formation. They also promote integration of the four dimensions of formation, allow a man's gifts to emerge, and point to areas where skills and virtues need to be developed.

Most of the information regarding a seminarian's pastoral formation comes from the seminarian, other faculty, and reports by his various supervisors. Reviewing these reports with a seminarian, whether it be from a summer assignment or current ministry can make for a fruitful discussion. For men in hospital ministry, discussing hospital experiences and reviewing verbatims make for rich conversations that can help a man integrate human, spiritual, and pastoral formation experiences. It is also helpful to review regular preaching evaluations the men receive during preaching class. It is important to remember that, for most, these are first-time experiences and that skill development happens gradually, often by building on what went well and focusing on one skill at a time.

In our multicultural context, seminarians will need to develop skills that will help them navigate and lead multicultural communities. With this in mind, a seminarian will benefit from understanding and appreciating the differences between high- and low-context cultures that we discussed above. This will enable him to negotiate the different cultures in his parish and allow him to act as a bridge builder in the parish. Acting as a bridge builder also demands that he become a man of discernment. There are times when a low context approach is called for and there are times when a high context approach is warranted. He must discern which situation calls for which approach. He must also help each culture to understand when that is and what is called for if they are to build one parish united in Christ by the power of the Spirit.

Accompaniment: Discipleship and Conforming to Christ the Shepherd and Servant

In this chapter, I have separated out the different ways a formator accompanies a seminarian according to the different dimensions of formation. In practice, these different dimensions of formation are experienced by the seminarian simultaneously. Formation is a process of integration.

Whatever he does in seminary, he brings his life story and experience with him. He is constantly attending classes, working to develop a spiritual life and engaged in ministry. Intellectual formation is the most immediate dimension of the process he must deal with. Human formation is perhaps the most important and pastoral formation the most meaningful. For the first two years of seminary, spiritual formation can seem to focus on gaining clarity regarding his vocation, but he must always be focused on growing as a disciple of Jesus.

Formation for the priesthood involves the singular journey of discipleship. To be a disciple of Jesus is to be a learner. To be a disciple is to be involved in a lifelong process of learning from Jesus, learning about Jesus, and participating in his life and mission. A disciple is a person called by Jesus to follow him, to learn about the kingdom of God, and to live from a deep relationship with Jesus. It is a personal and communal journey learned and lived out within the body of Christ. Seminary formation involves being formed as a missionary disciple who loves the master and is inspired by that love to lead others into the life Christ offers us. This means developing a personal friendship with Jesus. Through this friendship, a seminarian will internalize the spirit of the Gospel and share in Jesus' vision, attitudes, and mindset. Much of what happens as a man becomes a disciple of Jesus is discussed in spiritual direction. However, as the four dimensions of formation become more integrated in a seminarian's experience, his developing relationship with Christ and its impact on every area of formation will become part of his conversation in formation advising.

A formator accompanies a man through this process by listening to him and encouraging him. He listens for when and where a seminarian's relationship with Christ informs his approach to his studies, his view of himself, his image of God, and his prayer practices and ministry. Special attention can be given to the ways this relationship produces growing interior freedom from attitudes and behaviors that are contrary to Christian discipleship:

- Obsession with personal appearance
- Presumed theological and disciplinary certainty
- Narcissism and the tendency to dominate conversations
- External preoccupation with the liturgy
- Inability to listen
- Careerism

At the same time, he will pay attention to a man's growth in the fruits of the spirit and Gospel virtues such as:

- Faithfulness, integrity, wisdom
- A welcoming spirit
- Patience, kindness, humility, and compassion for God's People.

When a seminarian has gained clarity about his vocation, he will have more energy to focus on being formed into a disciple of Jesus Christ.[17] The process of becoming a disciple of Jesus is a lifelong process that begins with baptism. A

---

17. *Ratio*, Introduction # 3.

seminarian who has arrived at this point in the formation process has been growing as a disciple for years but now can begin an intense period of growth as his discipleship is oriented towards priesthood. As a seminarian shifts his focus, the way a formator accompanies him changes.

Formation at this stage also involves a man gradually conforming himself to Christ the Good Shepherd and Servant. The goal of this stage is to become a gift of self for others and a sign of God's love for each person through his union with Christ. Conformity to Christ requires a profound contemplation of the person of Jesus Christ.[18] Consistent contemplation of Jesus in the Gospels will make a seminarian's relationship with Jesus more intimate and personal. He will discover that Jesus' mission was to gather God's scattered sheep, lead the people into the kingdom of God, and accompany them along the way by feeding them and caring for them.[19]

There are at least four ways a formator can recognize that a seminarian is beginning to reflect the likeness of Christ the Good Shepherd and Servant. First, the seminarian will begin to adopt the posture of a servant. By servant, I do not mean servile. He is to adopt the posture of a servant that Jesus lived. Throughout his ministry, Jesus acted in the service of the kingdom of God and in the service of the people of God by healing them, forgiving them, feeding them, and calling them to be part of the renewed people of God. He served them by giving of himself, eventually taking the form of a slave with his total gift of self on the

---

18. *Ratio*, 68.
19. *Ratio*, 37, 69.

cross. A seminarian moves toward serving others as Christ did when he seeks to serve Christ by serving the needs of God's people in self-giving love that conforms to the will of God. A formator will notice signs of a man's generosity as he offers himself to various seminary activities. His ability to be a servant leader will emerge as he takes on leadership roles in the house. After diaconate ordination, a seminarian will have many opportunities to practice servant leadership in various liturgical situations.[20]

Second, he will become a man of discernment. He will develop the ability to recognize his own motivations and desires while opening himself to the truths of life. He will be a man of prudence and discretion. As a man of discernment, he will also be able to discern the various spirits at work in his life and in the parish community. He will learn how to discern God's will. This will enable him to see God at work in the lives of the people of God. In addition, he must become an expert in pastoral discernment listening deeply and employing good judgment. He must always be listening to God and God's Word, trusting that the Spirit guides the Church.[21]

Third, like Jesus the Good Shepherd, he will work to know God's people, seek out the lost, and give his life for them.[22]

Finally, he will begin to develop pastoral leadership skills marked by compassion, generosity, and love for all, especially the poor. He will learn to exercise leadership in a spirit of peace and attentive accompaniment in all situations.[23]

---

20. *Ratio*, 38–39.
21. *Ratio*, 43, 120.
22. *Ratio*, 69.
23. *Ratio*, 119–20.

Conclusion

Throughout this chapter, I have been describing the different ways a formator accompanies a seminarian through the formation process and what each form of accompaniment requires of the formator. Each form of accompaniment always involves listening, asking questions, making observations, and offering feedback in a spirit of care and kindness. This is true when as the formator seeks to know and understand the seminarian, when he helps him with a human formation issue or accompanies him through his discernment, his pastoral development, and his growth as a disciple and good shepherd.

4 | Forming of the Heart and the Imagination

THE LAST CHAPTER OFFERED concrete suggestions for how a formator can accompany a man through the four dimensions of formation. The goal of that process is the transformation of the heart and mind of the seminarian into a disciple of Jesus who reflects the heart and mind of Christ the Good Shepherd and Servant. There is an approach to formation advising that can undermine this important work that happens when a formator takes a superficial approach to formation advising by treating the advising meeting as a superficial check-in or a report on tasks the seminarian needs to complete. This approach misses the deeper realm of experience where the Lord is at work and where real formation occurs. It ignores how much every seminarian has already been formed and deformed by the time he enters seminary. Nor does it consider that real formation and transformation occur on the deep and vast realm of experience that is below the level of the tasks we seek to complete. This superficial approach causes a formator to miss where and how the seminarian needs to be healed and freed. He can miss where and how the various dimensions of formation are transforming this man and where and how the Lord is at work in his life.

This chapter invites formators to pay attention to the deeper parts of the seminarian's life in their approach to formation advising. Drawing on the work of contemporary cognitive psychologists, I set out some key features of the deep and complex internal world that every seminarian brings to formation. This will lead formators to pay attention to a seminarian's desires, imagination, and habits as a way of engaging the deeper realm of experience where real formation occurs. Although this chapter is less practical than the others, nevertheless, the material covered here offers a solid basis for the practical approach to formation suggested throughout this handbook. As a person gains experience as a formator, he begins to ask, what am I doing? What part of a seminarian am I aiming to form and transform? This chapter seeks to address those deeper questions.

Deeper Listening: The Heart and the Imagination

The deeper dimension of a seminarian's life is found in his heart, his deepest desires, and in his imagination. It is this deeper dimension of a seminarian's experience where formation occurs. This is the area of a seminarian's experience that a formator must pay attention to in formation advising. The reason for focusing on the heart, desires, and imagination is that as human beings we are primarily lovers rather than thinkers or doers. We are defined not by what we know but by what we desire, especially by our deepest desires. Simply put, we are what we love. This understanding of the human person is supported by recent developments in philosophy, neuroscience, and cognitive psychology. Much of this research has been pulled together by the philosophical theologian James K. A. Smith in his remarkable three-volume study on the process of forming Christian disciples.[1] In those volumes, Smith argues that formation for Christian discipleship should focus more on the heart than the head, more on desires and imagination than on beliefs, or tasks to be completed. When a formator pays attention to a seminarian's desires and imagination, he can direct the seminarian to these parts of himself as well. Drawing on Smith's work, I will explain why the heart, desires, and the imagination need to be the focus of formation advising.

All formation operates under an assumption about what it means to be human. The formation program that emphasizes study, assumes we are primarily thinking beings. The program that emphasizes pastoral practice and other activities, assumes we are doers. This handbook follows the research set out by James Smith and assumes human beings are what we love. What we long for and desire defines who we are. We are hearts more than heads or hands. By heart, I do not mean merely the place where our feelings originate in the modern romantic sense of the word. I am following the biblical understanding of the heart as the center of our

---

1. James K. A. Smith, *Desiring the Kingdom: Worship, Worldview and Cultural Formation*, Volume 1 (Grand Rapids: Baker Academic, 2009); *Imagining the Kingdom: How Worship Works*, Volume 2 (Baker, 2013); A more popular presentation of this material is found in James K. A. Smith, *You are What You Love: The Spiritual Power of Habit* (Grand Rapids: Brazos Press, 2016.)

consciousness and identity. It is where our deepest desires reside and where our decisions are made. The prophet Ezekiel understood the heart to be the focus of formation when he prophesied that God will take our hearts of stone and replace them with hearts of flesh, and pour his Spirit into us. St. Augustine echoed this view of the human person when he claimed that our hearts are restless until they rest in God. Everyday human experience affirms that we are more feelers than thinkers or believers. We make our way through the day effortlessly without needing to think through each move we make. We wake up, brush our teeth, walk through our house, and drive to work for the most part without thinking about it. When we do this, we are tapping into our unconscious understanding and feeling for things to navigate daily life.[2]

An approach to formation that privileges the heart fits with the *Ratio*'s emphasis on discipleship as the key to formation. When the disciples approached Jesus at the beginning of John's Gospel, he asked them "what do you want?" (John 1:38) At the end of John's Gospel, he asks Peter "Do you love me?" (John 21:16) He does not ask them what they know or believe. Discipleship is more a matter of hungering and thirsting than knowing and believing. It is about aligning our loves and desires with Jesus and his kingdom. It is about conforming our will to his will so we desire what God desires. Being a disciple of Jesus calls for a pure heart and an imagination shaped by the coming kingdom of God.

Focusing on the heart means paying attention to a seminarian's desires. It is our many desires and longings that drive most of our decisions and actions throughout the day.

---

2. See Smith, *You are What You Love*, 1–25.

We are driven by physical and emotional desires. We are motivated by a desire for meaning, truth, power, and respect. These many desires and longings reside in the heart.³ Now many of our desires are trivial, such as our love for chocolate ice cream or our desire that the Yankees win. But there are deeper more ultimate desires that orient our life and shape how we are in the world. These deeper desires are what fill us with passion and give our life direction and meaning. They drive us to "act in certain ways, develop certain relationships, pursue certain goods, and make certain sacrifices."⁴ The former superior general of the Jesuit order, Pedro Arrupe expresses the central role the heart plays in a person's life:

> Nothing is more practical than finding God,
> than falling in Love in a quite absolute, final way.
> What you are in love with, what seizes your imagination,
>   will affect everything.
> It will decide what will get you out of bed in the morning,
>   what you do with your evenings, how you spend your weekends,
> what you read, whom you know, what breaks your heart,
> and what amazes you with joy and gratitude.
> Fall in Love, stay in love, and it will decide everything.⁵

The heart functions as part compass and part engine. As a compass, it directs a person toward the image of the

---

3. Smith, *Desiring the Kingdom*, 46–50.
4. Smith, *Desiring the Kingdom*, 52.
5. "Fall in Love," Prayer Video, Ignatian Spirituality, accessed October 12, 2019, https://www.ignatianspirituality.com/fall-in-love-prayer-video.

good life and of human flourishing he received from his culture and society. Every person carries this image within his imagination. It expresses what happiness and human flourishing look like. It shapes our expectations and assumptions about life, particularly what we expect relationships to look like, what counts for work, what flourishing families look like, and more.[6] The heart is also like an engine filled with desires that drive us toward this vision of the good life. The attractive and alluring power of this vision captures imagination and evokes in us powerful desires. We are drawn toward it. It directs our desires and decision. It is what we want and crave. This is how we are oriented to the world by what we desire and love.[7]

I mentioned that this image of the good life is carried by our imagination. The imagination is a pre-cognitive faculty by which we navigate and make sense of our world. It is not our ability to be inventive or fantastic— the stuff of make-believe creativity. It functions like an invisible map we unconsciously consult all the time that provides us with an implicit guide for navigating everyday life. It shapes how we perceive and evaluate ourselves, others, and God. Most of us go through life unaware of this orienting map until we find ourselves in a very different culture and suddenly, we cannot make sense of things. This can also happen when we meet someone who has a very different vision of the good life than ours. Only then do we realize this map exists.[8] A major task for formators is to help a seminarian discover what this

---

6. Smith, *Desiring the Kingdom*, 52–53.
7. Smith, *Imagining the Kingdom*, 124–26; 137–39.
8. Smith, *Imagining the Kingdom*, 17–19.

assumed image of the good life looks like and how it squares with the kingdom of God.

The everyday rituals and routines that make up the practices of our life are driven by what we love and desire. These daily practices eventually form into dispositions, habits and a perception of the world from which our actions flow. It is important to stress that the loves and desires that orient our life operate most of the time without our thinking about it. They operate like an unconscious desire. They constitute the default orientation we take for granted most of the time. When we follow the invisible map that leads to the good life, we operate from a set of virtues or vices that corresponds to the given view of the good life. We develop these habits through various daily practices that make them automatic. These practices form our desires and shape how we love.[9]

Already Formed and Deformed

Long before a man enters seminary, he has been formed by his family of origin, his educational experience, his experience of church, and ultimately our consumer culture. These various actors have promoted a vision of the good life and of human flourishing that is deeply embedded in his imagination. He unconsciously internalizes the values, assumptions, and behaviors of these formative forces by engaging in every day routines, rituals, and practices, such as eating dinner with family, shopping, watching a football game, going to church, texting a friend, or swiping through a dating application. These practices seem innocent enough, but

---

9. Smith, *Imagining the Kingdom*, 157.

they are very formative. They promote a vision of the good life by telling compelling stories and presenting powerful symbols of the good life. These stories and symbols make powerful implicit claims about human flourishing and happiness. This is why companies do everything to promote and protect their brands.[10] We tend to surround ourselves with people who share this vision and reinforce our belief in it. As we do so, it seeps into our bones. As it inspires our decisions and actions, it begins to shape our character and identity.[11]

The ways in which a person is formed by family, the nation, church, and consumer culture would each require a book-length discussion. I will provide a few words on each to alert formators to the ways these influences form seminarians long before they arrive at seminary. Our nation promotes a set of values through the stories it tells, the symbols and rituals it promotes that causes us to absorb its vision of the good life. A nationalistic and patriotic vision of life is regularly promoted by movies, songs, and rituals like standing for the national anthem and celebrating Fourth of July. They contain a story of freedom and national unity that demands allegiance and loyalty and regularly calls for sacrifice even to the point of giving one's life for the country. Formators will want to help seminarians reflect on this formation in the light of the Gospel and Catholic social teaching.

Another formative influence on a person entering seminary is his prior religious experience and his experience

---

10. Smith, *Desiring the Kingdom*, 75–88. Smith analyzes how the mall, stadium, and college campus are formative of our desires and image of the good life, 89–129.

11. Smith, *Desiring the Kingdom*, 54–55. For more on this, see James H. Olthuis, *The Beautiful Risk: A New Psychology of Loving and Being Loved* (Grand Rapids: Zondervan, 2001), 68–70.

of Church. Men come to seminary with assumed images of God, Jesus, priesthood, ministry, the spiritual life, and the Church. Formators will need to learn what those are and help him to reflect on them in the light of his theological studies. Most seminarians are not critically aware of how these images square with Scripture and our rich and varied theological traditions. This can make for interesting and, at times, challenging discussions.

It can be argued that consumer culture is the dominant formative force in Western culture. More than anything else, it forms and deforms our desires and our vision of human flourishing and human happiness. Consumer culture is the water we swim in. We take it for granted without noticing how formative it is.[12] It trains us to value appearance and what a person has achieved, especially through financial gain and power. It is the rich, beautiful, and famous who are revered in this culture. These people, we are told, have friends, joy, and love. This is the kind of life we are trained to desire. There is, of course, a sharp contrast between the glamorous vision of the good life as it is found in advertisements, sit-coms, and movies and the reality of daily life. The people in those ads and movies have what I do not have but want. Since I do not have what they have, something must be missing and wrong with me. If I just buy this product, I will be whole and happy. But the emptiness re-emerges not long after the product is purchased. Consumer culture also fosters competition among friends and colleagues. Since

---

12. Two important books on this subject are by William T. Cavanaugh, *Being Consumed: Economics and Christian Desire* (Grand Rapids: Eerdmans Publishing, 2008) and Vincent T. Miller, *Consuming Religion: Christian Faith and Practice in a Consumer Culture* (New York: Continuum Publishing, 2004).

we are valued by our appearance and not our character, we are in an endless competition for appearing a certain way dictated by the whims of the current fashion trends. This competition reduces everyone to an object either of attraction or revulsion. Girls and women are objectified as bodies to be desired according to a certain standard.[13] Consumer culture, especially in the United States, plays a major role in racism and sexism in our society by reducing all things, especially African Americans, women, and girls, to a commodity to be sold or scapegoated for our country's ills.[14]

How can we be saved from our constant failure to match up, from the endless competition, and from the wound that comes by being objectified? Consumer culture offers us an answer, making it the problem and the solution. Shopping is construed as a kind of healing therapy that can help a person deal with the sadness and frustration of our broken world. The thrill of the purchase and the sheen of the new and novel products are supposed to offer us the happiness, pleasure and fulfillment we long for. It is a world of constant consumption that plays on our desire for more by offering us the next new thing. Consumer culture promises that every desire you have can be fulfilled right now with a click of a mouse or swipe of your finger. No waiting, no putting off, no self-restraint is necessary.[15]

---

13. For an eye-opening account of how this happens, see Sharon Lamb Packing, *Girlhood: Rescuing Our Daughters from Marketers Schemes* (New York: St. Martins, 2006).

14. For a well-documented indictment of the collusion between US economic institutions with slavery, see Edward E. Baptist, *The Half Has Never Been Told: Slavery and the Making of American Capitalism* (New York: Basic Books, 2016).

15. Miller, *Consuming Religion*.

As I mentioned above, our vision of the good life with its attendant desires, values, and habits resides in the unconscious. It remains largely hidden and unknown to the seminarian and formator unless the seminarian has lived for a time in a foreign country. This makes it difficult for the formator and the seminarian to know about them. This is what makes formation work so challenging. It is a matter of getting at the hidden, assumed world from which a person operates. This involves helping him to become aware of what constitutes his vision of the good life and the dispositions and desires that flow from it. Then a formator will encourage him to discern what is, in the light of the Gospel, distorted and deformed and needs to be abandoned, and what is true and good and needs to be further developed. This is why it is so important for a formator to get to know the seminarians he works with. The good news is that the vision of the good life promoted by the Gospel with its values and attitudes has also been internalized by a person entering the seminary. The entire seminary process offers him an intense course in this Gospel vision with practices such as communal and personal prayer and ministry to help him internalize the Gospel vision of life and human flourishing.

The Deep World Within

Throughout this discussion I mentioned that the heart, desires, and the imagination, influence how we live without our knowing it. The vision of the good life we live for and the desires that drive us operate in the unconscious. For further insight into this world, I turn to the work of cognitive psychologists and their insight into two different systems that work together in our brains all the time. One system is visible and easily recognizable and the other is hidden most of the time. The visible system is associated with our conscious activities. These are mental acts we are aware of, that require effort, and over which we have control, such as doing our taxes. The hidden system is traditionally called the unconscious or the adaptive unconscious. It operates quickly and automatically, while the visible system is slow and deliberate. The visible system is at work when we are reading directions or working on a math problem or learning a new language or piece of music. The hidden system of the unconscious is at work when we respond with fear to a scary movie and when riding a bicycle or driving a car becomes effortless. It acts like a second nature that allows us to respond and act quickly without thinking, especially in dangerous situations. It is a vast hidden world that operates underneath our consciousness. Our conscious and unconscious mental processes do different things. Both are at work all the time and can support and cooperate with each other.[16]

When a formator and seminarian meet for formation advising, each person brings his life history and a deep vast world both have little awareness of. Since the visible system is what a formator experiences when he is with a seminarian, it is important for him to become more aware of the hidden, unconscious system and its widespread impact on

---

16. Daniel Kahneman, *Thinking, Fast and Slow* (New York: Farrar, Straus and Giroux, 2011), 19–24; Timothy Wilson, *Strangers to Ourselves: Discovering the Adaptive Unconscious* (Cambridge, MA: Belknap Press, 2002).

behavior. The goal is to expand every formator's awareness of the depth and mystery at work within every seminarian he accompanies in formation. What formators must realize is that most of a person's everyday life is determined by mental processes put into motion by our environment that operate outside of conscious awareness. Every seminarian brings to formation advising a vast, hidden, and complex world he carries within him. This hidden world lies in the unconscious and has a powerful influence over his conscious actions.[17] For three decades, Professor John Bargh has been studying this world and its relationship to conscious thought and behavior.[18] He has identified three dimensions of this world: the hidden past, the hidden present, and hidden future. The relationship between this hidden world and our conscious self can be expressed by the image of a small island surrounded by a vast ocean. The island with its plants, trees, and animals represents our conscious self. The ocean surrounding the island with its hidden world teeming with life that only rarely comes to the surface represents our unconscious self. Another image for this relationship is that of a computer screen with its visible icons with all the software running in the background making it all work. The icons, images, and text we see on our computer represent the conscious, visible dimension of our brain, while the many software programs making the computer operate represent the complex activities happening in the unconscious, hidden system of our brain.

---

17. John A Bargh and Tanya L. Chartrand, "The Unbearable Automaticity of Being," *American Psychologist* 54, no. 7 (July 1999): 462–79.
18. John Bargh, *Before You Know It* (New York: Touchstone, 2017).

Recall the dual task of the formation advisor—to get to know the seminarian he works with and to help him grow in self-knowledge. Since much of what makes up a seminarian's experience is hidden to him and to the formator, it is important for every formator to have a general understanding of the chief activities happening in the hidden world. Thankfully, researchers such as Dr. Bargh can help us. Armed with that knowledge, a formator will know what to listen for and will be able to recognize actions from the hidden world when they make an appearance in a man's life.

The Hidden Past

Every person carries within his unconscious the long-hidden past. This includes his ancient evolutionary history, forgotten childhood, and the culture he grew up in. Our ancient ancestors lived in a world that was often far more dangerous than ours. We inherited from them the unconscious drive for physical safety and survival. We are born with two survival skills that operate from the unconscious. The first is the automatic reflex that helps us deal with the many-sided dangers of the world. This lightning-quick system recognizes threats to our safety and survival by generating involuntary emotions, such as fear and worry. It also releases the hormone adrenaline so we can either fight or flee. Secondly, survival in that dangerous world depended on our ancestors cooperating with those they trusted and being able to coordinate activities with them. Fear, worry, and cooperation were essential for survival since they needed to run from those who appeared menacing and work with those who seemed trustworthy. We come equipped with the ability to quickly evaluate who can be trusted and the ability to read the emotions of others.[19]

Another part of our hidden past comes from childhood. Every child is born with the capacity to bond with parents and family. Even though most people have no memory of what happened to them before the age of five, those experiences are retained in our implicit memory that is housed in the hidden system of the unconscious. They have an enormous impact on our capacity to trust others and develop friendships. As we discussed in an earlier chapter, a person develops a secure or insecure attachment depending on how his main caregivers related to him and met or failed to meet his needs at an early age. Researchers have found that those who experienced social warmth as infants had an innate tendency to develop social warmth and trust toward others. Those with an insecure attachment from a lack of social warmth as infants struggle to develop relationships and to trust others. But as we saw, a person with an insecure attachment can develop a secure attachment later in life. The point is that these experiences shape our assumptions about the world, our feelings towards others, and confidence in ourselves.[20]

Every infant learns the language, culture, and ideology of the country he is raised in. The cultural assumptions absorbed during childhood permeate our lives. Culture is like water to fish. We swim in it, take it in, and hardly notice it. Consequently, the unconscious learning every child engages in

---

19. Bargh, *Before You Know It*, 35–51.
20. Bargh, *Before You Know It*, 56–67.

plays an important role in character formation. Researchers have shown that children are like sponges that soak up the environment they are raised in. They take in and internalize all the explicit and implicit values, preferences, and assumptions expressed by family and their caregivers.[21] Much to the surprise of researchers, stereotypes and prejudice are embedded even before kids start school, especially when it comes to race, gender, and faith.[22] These long-learned values, assumptions, and prejudices are the kinds of things formators listen for as a man tells his story or speaks about his interactions.

The Hidden Present

In recent years, psychologists and neuroscientists have discovered that our unconscious performs many operations that make much of everyday life possible. This is the hidden present of our unconscious mind. It functions like a vast underground world of hidden software programs operating constantly. For instance, there is a program that makes us aware of where our body is all time. Another ensures that our motor skills are running. There is a language program that works instantly with memory to store and retrieve words, expressions, and their meaning for speaking, reading, and writing. There is a filtering program that helps us sort through the millions of pieces of information our five senses take in at any given moment.[23]

---

21. Bargh, *Before You Know It*, 72.
22. Bargh, *Before You Know It*, 85–92. See Michelle Alexander's discussion of implicit racism in *The New Jim Crow* (New York: The New Press, 2010), 103–06.
23. Wilson, *Strangers to Ourselves*, 19–24.

Researchers have found that our unconscious mind is constantly working 24 hours a day. Known as the Unconscious Thought Theory (UTT), researchers have found that the mind is working around the clock making judgments and decisions. For instance, our unconscious mind is constantly evaluating people and situations as good or bad, deciding if we like or dislike someone or some situation. This explains how we can have immediate reactions to people and experiences, such as food, sunsets, and other people without thinking about them. These unconscious and automatic reactions and evaluations signal to us whether we should stay or go, approach or avoid a person or situation.[24] At the same time, our minds are constantly working on problems we need to solve and goals we want to achieve. The part of the brain that was active when consciously learning remains active when our conscious mind was distracted or worked on something else. Study after study demonstrates that the unconscious is better at making decisions regarding complex and multidimensional problems than our conscious brain.[25]

There is another dimension of this research that is crucial to the work of formation. Researchers John Bargh and Tanya Chartrand point out that the kind of implicit learning we have been describing also happens unintentionally.[26] The process of learning things so they are automatic itself becomes automatic. From birth, we are immersed in all sorts of environments beginning with our families, schools,

---

24. Bargh, *Before You Know It*, 126–37
25. Bargh, *Before You Know It*, 160.
26. See John A. Bargh and Tanya L. Chartrand, "The Unbearable Automaticity of Being," *American Psychologist* 54, no. 7 (1999): 467–79.

sports teams, neighborhoods and workplaces. We are primed to unintentionally internalize attitudes and assumptions from that environment. This is how children learn their native language without studying it. It is how children learn they are loved. Through this process of unintentional learning, we develop implicit views of ourselves. It is how we develop our value system and how we perceive the world and internalize stereotypes. Every seminarian enters seminary having been immersed in the world of technology and consumer culture and the values associated with them. A large part of formation involves identifying the values and assumptions a man has learned from our culture and where they stand in the face of the values of the kingdom of God.

The unconscious plays an important role in how we learn and develop skills of all sorts. Any person who learned to play the violin, hit a baseball, drive a car, or speak another language knows how difficult these activities can be at first. However, with regular practice and coaching, they can become easy and automatic over time. As these skills become automatic, conscious choice drops out.[27] Neuroscientists tell us how this happens. When we try a new skill, fresh neural networks are created. With practice, these neural networks grow a fatty tissue called myelin to insulate the nerve fibers, increasing the speed, strength, and accuracy of the signal. As this happens, the skill or habit becomes automatic. After a certain amount of practice, the brain moves knowledge and skills we learn and develop from the conscious level to the vast storehouse of our unconscious. The brain constantly moves explicit knowledge, skills, and

---

27. Kahneman, *Thinking, Fast and Slow*, 19–24.

habits into our unconscious so that we can draw on them automatically. This saves the brain enormous amounts of energy. Musicians, athletes, and for anyone learning a new feature on their computer go through this process. Seminarians experience this when they learn to preach and learn how to lead a liturgical event. At first it can be quite taxing, but eventually much of it can be done automatically. This understanding of the movement from the conscious to the unconscious mind, from a difficult practice to it becoming automatic, can be a source of great motivation for seminarians learning new skills.[28]

The Hidden Future

Researchers have found that our mind is constantly working on our future. When nothing else is going on, our mind enjoys working on problems yet to be solved and on goals yet to be realized. This is the role the hidden future plays in our unconscious mind.[29] There are two ways the unconscious mind is oriented towards the future. The first involves future goals and desires each of us has. Who and what we want to be in the future shapes what we think, feel, and do in the present. We see the world through goal-colored glasses.[30] Often, our goals and long-term desires motivate us in unconscious and hidden ways while influencing much of what we do. For instance, we are driven to survive, mate,

---

28. For a helpful discussion of the role myelin plays in the formation of habits good and bad see Daniel Coyle, *The Talent Code: Greatness Isn't Born, It's Grown. Here's How* (New York: Bantam Books, 2009), 30–46.
29. Bargh, *Before You Know It*, 238.
30. Bargh, *Before You Know It*, 214.

be fed, be safe, belong, and socialize. When these goals are triggered by external influences, they can redirect what we pay attention to and even what we remember. They can even cause us to override many of our most cherished values and moral beliefs. It is important for formators to help seminarians identify the deeper goals and motivations that can drive their behavior.[31]

The second way our unconscious mind is oriented towards the future involves problems that need to be solved. Behind the scenes our mind is constantly working on our future—problems to be solved, goals to be achieved, insights to be discovered. Researchers have proposed different kinds of problems and puzzles to demonstrate just how good the unconscious is at solving problems. Many scientists, artists, and intellectuals have come to a new insight or have solved a problem while doing something else, or thinking about something else, or simply dreaming. This gives evidence for the advice of sleeping on it. It provides a reason for starting papers, homilies, and other projects ahead of time so the unconscious mind can work on them.[32]

I have been discussing the many dimensions of the hidden world that every seminarian and formator brings to formation advising. This hidden world contains deep influences from the past, present, and future that shape our behavior, our choices, our likes and dislikes. Most of us are unaware of these influences and activities that are constantly at work in our hidden self. By awakening formators to this hidden world, they will have a greater appreciation of the mystery

---

31. Bargh, *Before You Know It*, 214–29.
32. Bargh, *Before You Know It*, 239–56.

each seminarian brings to the formation process. They will be on the lookout for when and where that hidden world surfaces in a seminarian's experience and will thus be better equipped to help him grow in his self-knowledge.

Implications for Formation

The point of our exploring the heart, imagination, and the hidden unconscious world is to encourage formators to pay attention to the deeper dimensions of a seminarian's experience. There are important implications for formation worth noting from this discussion. The first is that every person who enters the seminary has already been formed by his family of origin and by our consumer culture. He comes in with only the tip of the iceberg visible and the rest of him still invisible and, in many cases, unknown to him. By getting to know about some of that vast hidden world, formators can help seminarians get to know themselves.

Second, the way a person is formed by his family of origin and from consumer culture can be contrary to the vision of human flourishing and happiness found in the kingdom of God as proclaimed and embodied by Jesus. In the light of the kingdom of God, the formation one received from family and our consumer culture can be a deformation and a distortion of one's desires, values, and actions. Consequently, a seminarian carries within him rival stories about the good life and contending visions of human flourishing. He will have contrary desires and longings struggling for dominance and attention in him along with contending dispositions and habits. These two visions of the good life produce contrary perceptions of the world. On the one hand, he has been trained to believe he is the center of all things, while the Church claims Christ is the center of the universe. Consumer culture has trained him in the practice of instant gratification and self-promotion, while the Gospel calls for self-denial and concern for the needs of the other. When we shine the light of the Gospel and the kingdom of God onto his previous formation, we start to notice how distorted his vision of the good life and human flourishing can be. Furthermore, the vision of the Gospel and the kingdom of God that he received thus far from the Church, may be distorted and deformed and in need or transformation.

Third, seminary formation must offer an intense, embodied experience of the kingdom of God as proclaimed and lived by Jesus Christ that will bring about a conversion of his imagination. All four dimensions of formation should promote an experience of the risen Jesus and the Spirit so that the seminarian internalizes the vision of the good life and human flourishing shaped by the coming of the kingdom of God and the dawning of God's new creation.[33] As he experiences the kingdom coming into his life through Christ and the Spirit and internalizes the story of the kingdom, a new view of himself and his relationships will emerge in human formation. This can happen through the liturgy, through communal prayer and personal prayer, and the retreats he attends. His studies should correct and clarify distorted

---

33. For more on this subject see, N. T. Wright, *Surprised by Hope: Rethinking Heaven, the Resurrection and the Mission of the Church* (New York: HarperOne Publishing, 2008); *Simply Good News: Why the Gospel is News and What Makes It Good* (New York: HarperOne Publishing, 2015); and *Surprised by Scripture* (New York: Harper One Publishing, 2014).

views of the kingdom of God, Jesus, and the Church. Meanwhile, his use of pastoral skills in ministry should gradually be informed and inspired by his experience of the kingdom and his growing vision of the kingdom of God.

Fourth, formation involves the purifying and redirecting of our desires and the sanctifying of our perception through the development of a new vision of self, others, God, the Church, Christian ministry, and creation. Unlearning old habits and attitudes will be part of this process. Discovering the vision of God's new creation coming through Jesus' resurrection and what it means for his priesthood and ministry is the other part. In short, seminary formation involves the reorientation and transformation of the imagination, desires, and one's perception of things so as to act in the service of the kingdom of God. For this to happen, seminarians will need to be immersed in the story of the Gospel as expressed by communal and personal practices, and rituals beginning with liturgy and communal prayer as well as community life, formation meetings, and retreats. They will need to put the Gospel into practice in their relationships in and outside of the seminary community. They will need to bring the Gospel to those they serve in ministry.[34]

Accompaniment and Deep Listening

The goal of this chapter has been to encourage a deeper and richer kind of listening by the formator of the seminarian's experience in order to help the seminarian learn about

---

34. In chapter 4 of *Imagining the Kingdom*, James K. A. Smith offers a discussion of how liturgy can reorient the imagination and sanctify our perception.

himself. I conclude this chapter with some suggestions for what to listen for in each of the dimensions of formation in the light of the material covered.

Human Formation

- Listen for his image of the good life by noticing where he finds meaning and fulfillment.
- Many men come to seminary suffering from a perfectionistic view of themselves. They hold onto a set of beliefs about how they are to live that they never live up to, thus generating frustration and potential self-hate. Formation advisors can help a man learn to accept himself and to like himself while growing comfortable with ambiguity. The hope is that they will one day discover they are loved by God.
- Listen to his experiences of relationships, past and present, and what they tell you about his orienting vision of his life.
- What desires and longings drive him?
- Has he begun to see life as a gift filled with mystery? Or is life still a series of tasks and obstacles to overcome?

Spiritual Formation

- What desires and longings drive his spiritual life?
- What assumed images of God, Christ, the Holy Spirit does he hold?
- What is his sense of the presence of God in his life and in creation?

- To what extent is he a person of gratitude?
- What is his image and experience (not understanding) of himself before God?
- What are his image and experience of sin, grace, salvation and the Church?
- What desires and hopes were present in his vocation story?
- How does he feel about celibacy?
- It is important to gain insight into his view of the Church. Some men arrive at seminary with a romantic view of the Church coupled with a great devotion to the Church. A chief task of formation is to help these men recognize the faults and sins of the Church, while cultivating a love for the church born out of a relationship with Christ and an experience of the people of God.

Intellectual Formation

- Listen for what drives him in his studies. Is he driven to achieve grades that are tied up with his image of himself?
- Some men are put off by the study of philosophy and theology. It is important to discover their attitude toward studies and the assumptions they bring to it. Often in reaction to the ambiguity and diversity found in the history of theology, students cling to ideology rather than theology. Formators can help seminarians move from seeing their courses as a source of information to approaching them as a means to transforming their theological, spiritual, and pastoral imaginations.

- Seminarians need help understanding what the role of theology is in their formation. Some treat their studies as any other set of graduate school courses with little connection to their spiritual life and ministry. Others can come to theology assuming their courses should be catechesis and information about the faith not knowing the difference between that and theology.
- A real challenge is to help seminarians see how their study of theology can impact their assumed images of God, Christ, the Spirit, and the Church and how they imagine God present in their life and the world.

Pastoral Formation

- How is he managing the transition from focusing on himself to being concerned about the needs of others?
- What desires drive his approach to ministry?
- What implicit images of ministry does he act from: a compassionate presence, the answer man, the one who wants to make everyone happy, a listener, or the one in charge?
- Listen for the various human formation issues that come up in pastoral ministry, especially in hospital ministry and preaching.
- Pastoral formation, whether it be service with the poor, hospital ministry, or preaching, brings with it great uncertainty and can promote a variety of reactions in a seminarian. Formators must pay attention as men describe their ministry experience. For many seminarians, ministry triggers fear and anxiety. Formation helps men

learn they are participating in the mission of Christ and all does not depend on them. This means moving men from fear to freedom and from power to service. This deep shift in approach to ministry requires integrating healthy pastoral theology and practices into their own approach to ministry.

5 | The Power of Participation

IN THIS HANDBOOK, I have been discussing the role the formator plays in the formation advising process. In this chapter, I turn to the seminarian and the active role he can play in his formation. Both John Paul II in *Pastoro Dabo Vobis* and Pope Francis in the new *Ratio* call on seminarians to be actively engaged in their formation. The more a seminarian takes an active role in his formation, the more it can transform him into a holy and healthy priest. Taking responsibility for his own growth and development in all four areas of formation is also an essential skill for life in the parish. There is a still deeper reason behind its impact on priestly life and ministry. When a seminarian is actively engaged in his formation, he is cooperating with the risen Lord who called him to this life and is the Formator. Realizing that the Lord seeks to form him into a disciple and transform him into his image can be a great source of motivation for a seminarian. He will be less likely to adopt a passive approach to formation or to view it as a matter of completing tasks. Instead, he will see it as an experience of discovery, of growing in freedom and self-knowledge. It will be a journey into who Christ wants him to become and how Christ wants him to serve God's people.

Formators must recognize that there is a power difference between themselves and the seminarians. This difference can put the seminarian in a passive and obedient posture. For a seminarian to become an agent of his formation and take responsibility for that formation, he must be given permission and even some guidance as to how to do this. Often seminarians come from formation programs where every step they take is dictated for them. Being asked to suddenly take an active role in formation can come as a strange shock to them. But there is real power in participation. Discovering the truth of this can require guidance and encouragement. This chapter discusses various ways a formator can promote a seminarian's active engagement with formation.

Fostering a Growth Mindset

When a seminarian takes an active role in his formation, he starts to develop what psychologist Carol Dweck calls a "growth mindset."[1] In her research into what motivates people to act, Dweck discovered two different ways people are motivated. The first group maintains a "fixed mindset." People with this mindset, whether they be students, athletes or employees, are motivated by a desire to receive recognition and approval. They are not motivated by a desire to grow and improve for its own sake. Dweck and her

---

1. Carol Dweck, *Mindset: The New Psychology of Success* (New York: Ballantine Books, 2008).

colleagues found that this group is less likely to take risks and try something new. They are afraid that if they fail, they will not receive the recognition they want. Failure is devastating for them. This approach undermines their ability to grow beyond their original promise.

The second group Dweck found manifested a "growth mindset." This group is motivated by the desire to improve. They are open to taking risks. Failure for them offers insight into areas they need to improve on. This is the mindset of the lifelong learner. It is the mindset that makes for a transformative experience of formation. The seminarian who takes charge of his formation will more than likely have a growth mindset. But it is quite easy for a seminarian to work for recognition rather than personal growth and advisors must be on the lookout for this difference in motivation.

Three concrete approaches to formation advising follow from Dweck's research. First, seminarians will benefit from a discussion of these two different mindsets. Most people live from one or the other without thinking about it. Those who already come with a growth mindset should be encouraged to continue with this approach. Those with a fixed mindset need to learn about the difference between the two mindsets and be encouraged to adopt the growth mindset.

Secondly, formators will find exploring what motivates a seminarian's approach to study, grades, and performance in preaching and ministry to be a fruitful conversation. It can help the seminarian uncover which mindset he holds. There are important human and spiritual formation issues that can be explored here. Beneath the question of motivation is the question of identity and self-worth. To what extent has a man heard the good news that he is loved by God and that his self-worth and identity are not tied to performance? To what extent is he seeking self-worth through performance and recognition from others? How and where does he find meaning? There are important formation issues to explore along these lines.

Thirdly, Dweck found that teachers and coaches can help cultivate a growth mindset in a person by praising effort rather than results. This may entail a change in how formators respond to what a seminarian does. Formators are so used to praising the result, such as a "great homily" rather than the effort it took to create that homily. Learning to encourage effort can have an impact on how a seminarian engages his formation. It leads to the seminarian seeking ways to grow and improve. Advising becomes a partnership in which we support, encourage, observe, and guide the progress a seminarian is making. Feedback is welcomed. Advisors who adopt a growth mindset will learn to explore with their advisee the process behind his successes and failures. The formator can help improve the seminarian's approach to formation by encouraging the seminarian to ask questions like where can I improve, what can I learn from this, and what can I change? These kinds of conversations will help the seminarian be conscious of what worked and help him to discover new ways of proceeding that can lead to growth next time.

One way to encourage a seminarian to take charge of his formation is by treating him as an adult. As an adult, he must keep his own schedule, take initiative in the seminary community, and cooperate with the formation process. This can be a challenge for some, especially if they come from a minor seminary where their day is dictated by a tight schedule. But eventually he will find it liberating. By learning to take charge of their own schedule in seminary and by taking an active role in their formation, they will be prepared to do this when they are ordained and when no one is there to dictate their schedule or demand they attend formation sessions. There is another reason to encourage men to take an active role in their formation. As the men take initiative and become responsible for their own formation, they begin to internalize what is happening through the formation process. Rather than being defensive and suspicious of formation, these men learn to view their advisors and spiritual directors as part of a support team that fosters their formation towards priesthood. A long-term benefit of this approach is the creation of lifelong learners who continually seek to "upgrade" themselves depending on the challenges they face in priestly ministry.

Two areas where the development of a growth mindset is most important are human formation and preaching. The shift from a fixed to a growth mindset can transform how a seminarian approaches human formation. Instead of being driven by the fear of a formator finding his weaknesses and fears, a seminarian with a growth mindset will look at formation as a chance to learn about himself, grow in freedom, and find healing and wholeness. For a priest to learn how to preach in a way that connects the lives of the people with the Gospel, he will have to become a lifelong learner. He will need to take a growth mindset into his approach to preaching. Adopting a growth mindset will allow him to receive criticism and work to improve all aspects of his preaching. He will continually ask questions, such as how can I improve my preparation process, what are new ways I can organize my homilies to better deliver my message, what are the best Protestant and Catholic preachers doing, how can I improve my delivery, and how can I better connect with the people?

The Practice of Regular Reflection

The seminarian who develops a growth mindset will also cultivate the habit of regularly reflecting on his life experience.[2] This wide-ranging practice will help him grow in self-knowledge. Regular meetings with a spiritual director, formation advisor, and a ministry supervisor offer opportunities to develop this habit. We live in a culture that drives us to focus on the next new thing and the next task to be done. Our culture does not train us to pause and reflect on our experience. But for seminarians and priests to move beyond a superficial task-oriented way of living, they must develop the prayerful practice of reflecting on all four dimensions of formation. This practice will help them make sense of their life, allow them to see the deeper movements in their life, recognize the way God is at work in their day, and help them learn how to handle difficult situations. For instance, to take an active role in human formation, seminarians need to reflect on their relationships past and present, on their emotional reactions in various situations, and on how well their way of relating to others is informed by the Gospel or not. It also includes reflection on their health, diet, and

---

2. *Ratio*, 58: "The seminarian is required to…review his own life constantly."

exercise. Intellectual formation requires a man to reflect on how he studies and handles the stress of studies, his attitude towards studies, and whether his studies are impacting how he envisions his spiritual life and ministry. Spiritual formation calls for regular reflection on his relationship to God, his prayer practices, how well he cooperates with the Lord, and how much he is or is not embodying the Gospel in his life. Pastoral formation calls for regular reflection on pastoral practice. This includes how well he listens, how he responds to God's people, and all dimensions of preaching. This kind of regular reflection will make for rich discussions in spiritual direction and formation advising.

The following questions can help a seminarian reflect on his experience.

- Consider your relationships inside and outside the house. Which were affirming and challenging? Were any strong feelings or memories stirred up? Did your actions and reactions conform with the life of a seminarian?
- Consider your studies. What new insights did you gain and what was challenging? How do you feel about your studies?
- Consider your spiritual life. What practices have you used in the past two weeks and have you been faithful to prayer, liturgy, and spiritual direction? Over the past two weeks, what has your relationship with God been like?
- Consider your pastoral ministry. What went well, and what was challenging?

Preparing for Formation Advising Meetings

A crucial way a seminarian can take responsibility for his own formation is by preparing for his formation advising meetings. Seminarians lead very busy lives as they try to keep up with their course work, attend the daily seminary events, get to their ministry site, pray, exercise, and socialize. They are under constant pressure to keep up with their readings and paper writing. The entire experience forces them to focus on the next thing that is due or the next event to attend. Pausing to step off this fast-moving train and reflect on their experience does not come naturally, and our American culture, and much of seminary life, does not promote it. The seminarian who does not pause to reflect on his experience of the previous two weeks will arrive at his formation advising meeting with little to say except to report on the tasks he has accomplished and the ones due soon. This makes for superficial and often boring conversations that compel the advisor to search for something substantial to discuss. He can feel like a man fishing with the hope of getting one bite! Contrast this with the seminarian who spends time before his meeting prayerfully recalling the main events of the past two weeks, his experience of those events, and, perhaps, where God was in them. He comes to advising with much to share! This makes for a rich, powerful, and interesting formation advising meeting. This seminarian has spent time exploring the deeper parts of his experience where real formation occurs and where God is at work.

Most seminarians will need guidance and support from the formator as to how to prepare for this meeting. I tell every seminarian I work with that preparation is required to work with me as a formation advisor. During our first meeting, I talk about how important it is that the seminarian prepare for our meetings. I ask him to put our advising meetings into his calendar and schedule time to prayerfully reflect on the previous two weeks before coming to our meeting. His reflection begins by recalling some of the events and experiences of the past two weeks and then goes deeper by noticing how he experienced these events and perhaps where God was found in them. Every experience is multidimensional and involves memories, feelings, desires, insights, and values. The practice of reflecting on his experience will expand his awareness of these many dimensions so he can understand them and act in a Christ-like way. By noticing his experience, he will begin to get in touch with the depth and meaning of his experience. This practice will help him learn about himself. It will also put him in touch with the places where Christ is most active in his life.

A description of this reflection process can be found in the seminary handbook that accompanies this one.

Formation Goal Setting Process

Another way advisors can encourage seminarians to take charge of their formation is by asking them to engage in a goal-setting process early in the fall semester.[3] It is not uncommon for seminarians to identify generic goals such as "I want to love God" or "I want to become a spiritual father" or "I want to make my entire day a prayer." Developing

---

3. This journaling process is based on material shared with me by Father David Thayer, PSS.

clearly defined, concrete goals with realistic strategies for attaining those goals will make a great difference in a man's formation. The seminarian handbook contains guidelines for a goal-setting process. This is a prayerful process of reflection that takes into account what is happening right now in their lives, the ways they have changed and grown in seminary, and where they are being called to grow in terms of the four areas of formation.

Implemented Intentions and Good Habits

Seminarians can participate in their own growth in formation by adopting two practices that are supported by years of research by cognitive psychologists. The first involves *implementing intentions*. Discovered and developed by psychologist Peter Gollwitzer of New York University, the practice of implementing intentions is a powerful way of ensuring a seminarian will carry out new goals and intentions that come up throughout the formation process. Whether it be a new goal for studies, exercise, prayer, nutrition, or ministry, the process developed by Gollwitzer is proven to put intentions into practice so they become a habit. The secret is to identify a future time, place, and way that a goal will be carried out. For instance, when trying to get a group of elderly people to take the various pills in the pillbox, researchers suggested they take pill 1 immediately after breakfast and pill 4 at bedtime right before turning out the light. Several months later the group had a 100 percent adherence rate. The same process was used for making doctor appointments, with voters, and with people who sought to avoid a temptation related to food. For instance, the dieters told themselves, "The next time I am tempted to eat chocolate, I will think of my diet." Researchers found this process was far more successful than willpower. The reason is that by linking the intended goal to a time and place, the person had an external cue that made the practice automatic. Brain imaging studies have shown that when implementation intention is employed, control over behavior shifts from the self-initiated part of the brain to the part of the brain stimulated by the outside environment.[4] Professor John Bargh reported using this method as a way of protecting his family from the frustrations of his workday. He succeeded in doing this by deciding when he gets out of his car before entering the house he would be happy he was home and about to be greeted by his family.[5] This is a powerful tool formators can share with seminarians as these men seek to make changes in each dimension of formation. The important point is to discuss with the seminarian the specific goal and the time and place where he will implement it. This process can be used for short-term goals.

The second approach involves a method for developing *good lifelong habits*. These lifelong habits include prayer, study, exercise, nutrition, and taking a day off that will help a priest live a healthy and holy life. Research shows that the best way to do this is to form good habits that are connected to a concrete place and time. At first, adopting a new practice, such as exercise, can be difficult, but by developing a regular routine, new neural pathways grow. As they strengthen

---

4. Peter Gollwitzer, "Implementation Intentions: Strong Effects of Simple Plans," *American Psychologist* 54, no. 7 (1999): 493–503.

5. Bargh, *Before You Know It*, 273–74.

through regular practice, the new practice becomes a habit. The good news is that the habit soon becomes part of behavior and not dependent on willpower. Researchers at the University of Pennsylvania found regular habits make an activity effortless, whether it be exercise, study, or any other habit. The trick is to set up one's environment so that it is easy to engage in the new habit. Setting out the breviary the night before so he prays it first thing in the morning, or associating study with the morning coffee, or setting out running shoes and shorts the night before all make a new practice easier and can turn it into a habit. By setting up the environment and making an implementation intention, the new practice soon becomes automatic.[6]

Reflection on Pastoral Practice

The most concrete way that a seminarian participates in the formation process is through his various pastoral ministry experiences. Most seminarians will be involved in the following kinds of ministry during seminary: ministry with the poor, catechesis, hospital ministry, and parish ministry. Men enter seminary with a desire to serve God and God's people, especially in the parish setting. While time consuming, ministry is often the most rewarding part of a seminarian's week. It can give a seminarian a sense that he is actively contributing to the ministry of the Church and bringing some good into people's lives.

---

6. Bargh, *Before You Know It*, 275–78; Brian M. Galla and Angela L. Duckworth, "More than Resisting Temptation: Beneficial Habits Mediate Relationships between Self-control and Positive Life Outcomes," *Journal of Personality and Social Psychology* 109, no. 3 (2015): 508–25.

Learning to reflect on these pastoral experiences is another important way a seminarian can participate in his formation. As I mentioned above, the practice of pausing to reflect on ministry experiences is not a natural habit in our task-oriented world that is focused on the next thing. Some men will not even understand the value of looking back at a ministry experience. Formators will need to explain how much a seminarian can learn about himself and his ministry by reflecting on his experience. Often, much more is happening than he realizes until a formator takes him through a guided reflection on the experience.

What follows are general questions a formator can use to lead a man to reflect on his ministry. They can also be given beforehand as an expansion of the process of preparing for the advising session.

- Progress: How is your ministry going thus far? What kinds of things are you doing? Let's consider a particular event.
- Gratitude: Looking back on your ministry experience, who and what are you grateful to God for?
- Mood: What mood were you in as the experience started? What feelings and desires emerged during and afterwards?
- Pastoral practice: What went well?
- The action of God: Where did you find God in this experience?
- Next time: Are there any ways to improve how you can serve God's people?

Reflection on Preaching

Most parish priests preach every day and each weekend. As countless surveys have shown, the people in the pew long for better preaching. Helping seminarians to reflect on their experience and practice of preaching is essential to forming good preachers who can transform lives by proclaiming the Gospel in engaging and meaningful ways.[7] This kind of reflection should happen while a man is enrolled in preaching courses. At different points during the semester, it is helpful to review with him what he is learning from his preaching class. This can lead to a conversation about how he prepares for a homily, how he felt while preaching, what he hoped to achieve and what response he received from his professor. The process of learning how to preach can be overwhelming and discouraging at first. Most men need encouragement. Growth occurs when he selects one area of the preaching process to work on per semester to improve his preaching. Once a seminarian is ordained a deacon, he will be preaching with some regularity in the parish. Reflecting on these experiences can be very fruitful as well. The following questions can guide some of this discussion.

- In a sentence, what was your message? What were you hoping the people heard?
- How did you feel while preaching?
- How was your eye contact? Were the people paying attention or were heads down?

---

7. A helpful resource for reflecting on different dimensions of preaching is Deacon Edward McCormack, "Ten Commandments for Transformative Preaching" in *Homiletic and Pastoral Review*, November 29, 2015. Found at www.hprweb.com.

- Describe your preparation process.
- How was your delivery?
- What feedback did you receive? What aspect of preaching do you want to work on improving this semester?

The Annual Seminarian Self-Evaluation

A very important way a seminarian participates in the formation process is by writing a thorough, insightful, and thoughtful self-evaluation. Whether a formator is working with a new or returning seminarian, it is helpful to discuss the purpose of the self-evaluation and what is expected. Most formators hand out a style sheet so there is a uniform presentation to the self-evaluations. Formators will find that a well-done self-evaluation helps them write their evaluations of each seminarian.

A self-evaluation invites a seminarian to reflect on and write about his formation experience in terms of the four dimensions of formation: human, spiritual, intellectual, and pastoral. It gives him an opportunity to look back on where he has grown in each area of formation, what have been the challenges, and what calls for further growth. A thoughtful and well-written self-evaluation will provide the formation faculty with evidence of his ability to reflect on his experience, acknowledge his gifts, and identify where he needs to grow.

When a formator receives a seminarian's self-evaluation, he reads it over and often sends it back for clarification or a fuller treatment of a topic. A style sheet and sample evaluation can be found in the accompanying seminarian handbook.

Conclusion

This chapter has stressed the crucial role that a seminarian plays in his own formation. He is a central agent in that process. Formators must learn to let go of their control of the formation process and allow seminarians to play an active role in the process. Seminary formation is about forming future leaders after all! There are many ways the seminary can provide opportunities for men to take an active role in formation. In this chapter, I have suggested various ways a formator can promote a seminarian's active contribution to formation advising. Certainly, goal-setting, preparing for formation advising meetings, and the self-evaluation are among the most important of these activities.

6 | Evaluations

A VERY IMPORTANT DIMENSION of formation advising is the practice of assessing a seminarian's gifts, emerging abilities, and areas for further growth.[1] This practice happens in an informal and formal manner. The informal evaluation of a seminarian happens as he lives in the seminary community, attends liturgy, and participates in community events. The formation faculty and fellow seminarians will notice how well a man gets along with others, the gifts he brings to seminary, and those that emerge as he goes through formation. Formation advising is a common place where seminarians can discuss their experience of this informal evaluation process. The formal evaluation process often begins with a fall review of each seminarian and culminates in the written evaluation in the spring. The goal of this chapter is to guide the new formator through the formal evaluation process. It begins with a discussion of bias and the ways it can distort any evaluation process. The rest of the chapter explains the various components of the evaluation process with a strong

---

1. *Ratio*, 58.

emphasis on writing the evaluation. Included here are guidelines for writing the evaluation, a style sheet, and sample evaluations for each year a man is in the seminary.

Bias in the Evaluation Process

Evaluating seminarians is more an art than a science. Most seminaries rely on the entire formation faculty to ensure a seminarian receives an honest and accurate evaluation. This is important because bias almost always plays a role in any decision and evaluation process. Psychologists Amos Tversky and Daniel Kahneman have spent their careers demonstrating how evaluations made by economists, doctors, and psychologists who claim to be drawing conclusions based solely on data are influenced by various biases.[2] The kinds of bias that influence these professions can also influence seminary formators.

The most important thing to understand about bias is that it emerges from the unconscious. Recall the distinction between the two systems operating in our mind: the conscious visible system and the unconscious hidden system. The bias that influences evaluating and deciding comes from the hidden unconscious system. It is not a conscious view one adopts but something that has been learned over time and resides in the unconscious. Our brain is able to absorb all sorts of cultural assumptions from family, Church, education, and popular culture. We take in these assumptions through images, stories, and various experiences. Most of these assumptions move quickly from the conscious experience to our hidden

---

2. The results of their research are summarized in Kahneman, *Thinking, Fast and Slow*.

unconscious world. Our unconscious, psychologists tell us, is the vast storehouse of memories, images, and assumptions that have an important and powerful impact on the decisions we make. It regularly provides impressions that can turn into beliefs, impulses that influences choices, quick judgments, and tacit interpretations about all sorts of things. That is often called implicit bias.[3]

The most common forms of bias that impact the process of evaluating a person are as jumping to conclusions, confirmation bias, the halo effect, the spotlight, stereotypes, and overconfidence in the future:

Jumping to Conclusions

Our mind is a meaning-making organism. When shown words with missing letters or sentences with missing words, the mind will automatically fill in the needed letters or words to make sense of what we are seeing. Similarly, our mind will generate a likely context when an explicit or a complete context is absent. This necessary and helpful ability can lead a person to make intuitive judgments about many things he knows little about. It causes us to jump to conclusions based on limited evidence. Formators can easily fall prey to this common trap.[4]

Confirmation Bias

Kahneman found that the hidden unconscious system will believe almost anything. Rather than testing claims and

---

3. Kahneman, *Thinking, Fast and Slow*, Part 1.
4. Kahneman, *Thinking, Fast and Slow*, 79–86, 96.

seeking data to confirm or deny a claim, it seeks data that is compatible with beliefs already held. It tends to favor uncritical suggestions. This is known as confirmation bias. Formators who jump to conclusions about a seminarian and then look to confirm what they believe need the kind, but critical input of other faculty members. They also need to be wary of this tendency and counteract it by seeking input from multiple sources.[5]

Halo Effect

Another form of bias is known as the halo effect. The hidden unconscious places a great deal of weight on the emotion attached to a first impression to the point of ignoring subsequent information or becoming blind to what is there. Formators must be aware of the bias developing towards those seminarians who are friendly, attractive, bright, and make a good first impression. (This also happens with teachers when a student does well on a first test. The halo effect can impact how the teacher views the student the rest of the semester.) The halo effect also works with regard to how one faculty member can influence the rest of the faculty by speaking early and assertively in a faculty meeting. The halo effect can sway all to his side and discourage them from being open to other independent views. This can have serious implications when a faculty is discussing a seminarian.[6]

---

5. Kahneman, *Thinking, Fast and Slow*, 81.
6. Kahneman, *Thinking, Fast and Slow*, 82–84.

The Spotlight or Narrow Frame of Reference

As we saw above, the unconscious hidden system of the brain will jump to conclusions based on limited evidence. It is also swayed by first impressions. This leads to the next form of bias known as "spotlight" bias where a person believes that what he sees is all there is to see. We perceive what is close and available without considering what we do not know about a man. When evaluating a seminarian, we can fall into the trap of believing that what we know about him is all there is to know about him. One-sided evidence has a powerful influence on our judgments. We must always remember that there is far more than what we know about any individual.[7]

Stereotypes

This is where implicit stereotypes can have a powerful impact on our judgments about a seminarian. Every formator holds an implicit set of assumptions about what makes for a good priest. These cover appearance, personality, character, and behavior. We hold onto these even though we know there is no one view of the priesthood.[8]

Overconfidence about the Future

Another bias a formator must be aware of involves overconfidence when it comes to predicting the future. Since the

---

7. Kahneman, *Thinking, Fast and Slow*, 85–88.
8. Kahneman, *Thinking, Fast and Slow*, 420.

adaptive unconscious is a meaning-making machine, it is inclined to see patterns everywhere, blinding us to irregularities. This is another reason we tend to jump to conclusions. A formator may, after noticing a few isolated events, jump to a conclusion rather than testing to see if these instances are related. A related danger is to assume that a current pattern of behavior is an accurate prediction of future behavior. Sports announcers regularly claim a player has a "hot hand." Teachers claim he was always a "bad egg." But as Kahneman and other researchers have shown, a small sample of events or actions is no predictor of the future. Formators beware! A few actions in seminary do not predict how a man will fare as a priest.[9]

Fall Review

In many seminaries the formal evaluation process begins in the fall when the formation faculty conducts a review of each seminarian. This offers each formator a chance to pause and consider how each of his advisees is doing thus far and what may be the chief formation issue each man is working on this year. The fall review gives the entire faculty a chance to get to know each seminarian, especially the new men. At the same time, it provides a way for each formator to gain insight into the men they work with by receiving input from the rest of the faculty. Generally, these are brief "snapshots" of each man. It is common practice to share with the faculty a brief biographical background of all men who are new to the seminary.

---

9. Kahneman, *Thinking, Fast and Slow*, 114–18.

Pre-Evaluation Conversation

When spring evaluation time comes around, formators often devote part of a formation meeting to a pre-evaluation conversation. At this point, the seminarian should have begun to think about his own self-evaluation. When a formator invites a seminarian to reflect on the year and where he has grown in the four dimensions of formation, a wonderful and insightful conversation often ensues. As he reflects on his experience from August until the present, most seminarians will touch on the four areas of formation. A formator may have to prime the pump a bit by asking about a man's prayer practices, where he stands with his vocation, with celibacy, or how has his ministry has been. But in most cases, little promoting will be needed.

Some formators strike while the iron is hot and write down much of what the man shares so that this information can go into the evaluation. This will speed up the writing process. By inviting the seminarian into this reflection process, a formator is demonstrating to the seminarian the importance of his participation in the evaluation process. By asking and recording the answers to the following questions, a formator will be well on his way to writing an evaluation.

Introduction
- How old are you?
- Have you been instituted as an acolyte and reader?

Biographical Background
- What are the names of your parents, brothers, or sisters?
- Where did you grow up?

- Where did you attend college?
- Any work experiences?

Human Formation
- How was your experience of the community this year?
- Who would you consider your friends?
- What do you do for recreation?
- In what ways do you contribute to the life of the house?
- What committees were you a part of?
- What have been the main formation issues you have worked on this year?
- Where have you grown?
- In what areas have you struggled?

Spiritual Formation
- How would you describe your participation in the community liturgy?
- What spiritual practices do you engage in?
- Do you participate in the sacrament of reconciliation?
- How often do you see your spiritual director?
- How are you feeling about your vocation and your commitment to chaste celibacy?

Intellectual Formation
- What degree programs are you enrolled in?
- What courses have you enjoyed?
- Did you make any connections between your courses and spiritual life and ministry?

Pastoral Formation
- Where are you in ministry this year?
- What were your duties?
- What did you learn?
- Where did you grow in your understanding of yourself, the people of God, and in your ministerial skills?

Guiding the Seminarian's Self-Evaluation

At the beginning of January, the formation faculty receives a schedule listing when each seminarian's evaluation will be voted upon. This gives the formator time to think about each man he works with and write an evaluation that reflects the ways the seminarian has grown in the past year and where he still needs to grow in his formation toward priesthood. Based on this schedule, the formator should inform his advisees about when their self-evaluation is due. The newer men tend to be evaluated later, which allows them to include in their self-evaluation experiences from the early spring semester, such as their retreat, the transition back to seminary, and their ministry with the poor.

Guidelines for how a seminarian should write his self-evaluation can be found in the seminarian handbook. The evaluation should be a well-written and thorough reflection of his experience in formation using as a guideline the four dimensions of formation and the goals he set for the year. The evaluation should exhibit the seminarian's growing self-knowledge and insight into his experiences, especially his struggles and where he has grown in each dimension of formation. Formators should read and review the evaluations before sharing them with the rest of the faculty. A self-evaluation may be sent back to the seminarian asking him to provide more depth of thought and insight into his experience.

Writing the Seminarian's Annual Evaluation

The task of writing seminarian evaluations is an essential part of the formation process. Each formator writes an evaluation about each seminarian he works with in formation advising. The evaluation should be an accurate reflection of where and how a man has grown during the year in the four dimensions of formation in the light of the goals he set at the beginning of the year. Each evaluation is reviewed and approved by the formation faculty and is sent to the bishop in the name of the rector. The evaluation should be written in a professional manner while demonstrating a personal knowledge of the seminarian. To ensure a professional product, a standard format is employed and, at certain points in the evaluation, a standard set of expressions are used. This procedure aids in the writing of accurate, informative, and readable evaluations.

Faculty Evaluation Style Sheet

Font:	Times New Roman
Font Size:	12 point
Line Spacing:	Single spaced
Punctuation Spacing:	Two spaces
Pagination:	No pagination
Section Headings:	Bolded, not underlined
Paragraph Indentation:	No indentation, flush left, block style

Sample Evaluation

The following sample of an evaluation indicates the kind of information each section of the evaluation is expected to contain. The introduction and recommendation contain examples of the standard language used at certain points in the evaluation.

Faculty Evaluation of N

(Seminarian's First and Last Name no middle names, bolded)

Fall or Spring, Year

Introduction

- The standard format for introduction to an evaluation is as follows: *X, a twenty-four-year-old seminarian sponsored by the Arch/diocese of X, is in his second year of formation at Theological College and his second year of theology at The Catholic University of America.* (If the seminarian has a preferred nickname, list his given name first, then his nickname. For the remainder of the evaluation his nickname may be used, i.e., John "Jack" Smith.)
- If the seminarian has been instituted as a lector and/or acolyte, include that with a comment on his performance. (The date of institution is not necessary). The standard expression of this is: *X was instituted into the ministries of Acolyte and Lector and faithfully fulfills these ministries.*
- If a seminarian is an ordained deacon, he is introduced as "Reverend Mr."

- If the seminarian has received candidacy, note that in the introduction.
- The introduction concludes with the faculty's recommendation for advancement to the next stage of formation. It can be stated this way: *This evaluation will review his formational progress during the year and conclude with a recommendation that X be advanced to second theology in the fall.*
- If a man is recommended for candidacy, formulate the recommendation as follows: *This evaluation will review his formational progress during the year and conclude with a recommendation for Candidacy.*

Biographical Background

This section of the evaluation is only necessary for students who are *new* to seminary during the academic year. It should contain a brief overview of the student's formative years including where he was born and grew up, his parents, their marital status, where he was in formation prior to entering major seminary, and any other *pertinent* formative history. A few words about his vocation story may be included as well.

Human and Spiritual Development

Begin this section with a few sentences describing what the seminarian is like as a person. Include the kinds of relationships he has inside and outside of the seminary and the ways he participates in the life of the seminary and contributes to seminary community.

Describe how he approaches formation advising meetings. Describe his relationship with his advisor and his approach to advising and formation. Set out the issues discussed in advising and the main human formation goal he worked on this year. Capture where growth has occurred, effort was made, and where further growth may be needed.

This section should be a brief paragraph indicating the seminarian's participation in the daily liturgy, his regular habit of praying the Liturgy of the Hours, receiving the sacrament of reconciliation, and his meeting regularly with his spiritual director. Identify personal spiritual practices and spiritual goals.

For men who are moving toward ordination to the diaconate, indicate the seminarian's desire and readiness for obedience, chaste celibacy, his commitment to prayer and the Liturgy of Hours, as well as simplicity of life. Also comment on his understanding of what he is committing to and why he thinks he is ready for this kind of commitment.

Intellectual and Pastoral Development

This section should contain a brief paragraph indicating the academic program the student is currently enrolled in (i.e., M.Div., dual M.Div./STB). Mention should be made of the student's fall and current cumulative GPA. Describe what type of student he is, what courses he enjoys, and any intellectual gifts or struggles.

This section begins with a brief discussion of his experience of last summer's ministry assignment. Then discuss his current pastoral placement with pertinent quotations from the student's self-evaluation and pastoral supervisor, especially if he is enrolled in Basic Supervised Ministry, Preaching I and II, and when a seminarian in Third and Fourth Theology is serving in a parish. Mention should be made of emerging pastoral gifts and areas for further growth.

Recommendation

This section presents the commendations from the faculty for ways in which the seminarian may have improved or grown during the past year. Encouragement can be offered regarding areas for growth and improvement to be attended to during the summer and coming year. The recommendation for advancement is included here.

The recommendation section usually includes the following: (1) an acknowledgment of the contributions the man has made to the house, (2) an invitation to work on a growing edge that emerged during the year, and (3) a recommendation to move on to the next stage of formation. The recommendation can be stated as follows: *The faculty commends X for... They appreciate...They encourage him... Therefore, the faculty recommends...*

The following are examples of a recommendation for each stage of formation:

- Recommending a Basselin scholar return:
  Therefore, the faculty recommends that X continue in the Basselin Scholars program when he returns to Theological College in the fall.

- Recommending men for candidacy completing their second year of formation:

    Therefore, the faculty recommends that X be admitted to Candidacy and he return to Theological College to complete his formation for priesthood.
- Recommending a man to candidacy who is going on a pastoral year:

    Therefore, the faculty recommends that X be admitted to Candidacy and he return to Theological College to complete his formation for priesthood upon successful completion of his pastoral year.

Troubleshooting

The language used in an evaluation should be clear and professional. The following are reminders toward that end and a list of expressions to avoid.

Grammar Reminders
- Avoid mixing tenses in the same sentence. If the paragraph begins with the past tense, *all verbs* should be past tense for the rest of the sentence.
- Use the active voice.
- When writing "St." for "saint" be sure to include the period after St.

Stylistic Reminders
- Avoid using the seminarian's name at the beginning of each paragraph.
- When writing more than one evaluation to the same

diocese, avoid using the same expression to describe a dimension of a man's formation in two different evaluations.

Capitalize and Italics
- Capitalize the word "Diocese."
- When you italicize the name of an academic course in one part of the evaluation, all subsequent titles should be italicized.
- Capitalize the words "Acolyte," "Lector," and "Candidacy."
- All Latin expressions are lowercase italicized, i.e., "*lectio divina.*"
- When you capitalize "Bishop" once in a document, it should be capitalized throughout (with or without the name of the Bishop notated).

Corrections and Editing
- Incorporate changes recommended by the faculty and remember to save these changes.
- It is helpful to print out the evaluation, set it aside, and then return to make a final edit. This makes it easier to see and correct confusing sentences and expressions, i.e., *He feels more whole and fulfilled in a celibate vocation than as a married man.* A bishop or a panel is going to look at this sentence and ask, "How does he know? Has he been married?"

Expressions to Avoid
- Refrain from the following words: "gotten," "comfortableness," "baggage," "guys in the house," "happy-go-

lucky," "endearing," "seems," "powerless," "kids" instead of students, "church," and "docility."
- Refrain from using "unfortunately." If a student has endured a hardship, reference it plainly, i.e., if the student's grade suffered due to an unintentional issue with a citation on a term paper, state the details plainly and objectively. Using words like "unfortunately" adds a subjective assessment to the evaluation where it is not called for.
- Refrain from referencing advising meetings with the possessive "our meetings." This evaluation will eventually be formatted and *signed by the rector*, who does not have advising meetings with the student.
- Refrain from *naming individuals* in the evaluation other than the seminarian unless it is a direct quote from a pastoral supervisor. This includes naming other students, seminary staff, even a "co-captain" or "co-chair" and therapists. Too many names can clutter the document.

References to Avoid
- Refrain from making references to places and institutions in the local area since many who will read the evaluation will not be familiar with those references.
- Refrain from local area references a reader from outside the area may not know about. For instance, avoid mentioning the difficult commute a student makes from seminary to Georgetown MedStar Hospital.

More Sample Evaluations

Sample Faculty Evaluation of N

Spring, 20xx

N., a (age) seminarian sponsored by the Diocese of X, is completing his X year of theological studies at The Catholic University of America and his _____ year of formation at Theological College. Instituted as a Lector last year, he continues to faithfully and effectively exercise this ministry. This evaluation will review his progress during the past year and conclude with a recommendation_____.

Biographical Background

Include this material for all new students with a focus on family background, education and previous employment.

Human and Spiritual Development

- Note where he was last summer and how his transition back to seminary went. In a few sentences describe what he is like. Indicate that he has appropriate relationships inside and outside seminary. Mention any way he participates in the life of the seminary
- Describe how he approaches formation.
- Describe key formation issues.
- Mention goals and issues discussed and areas of growth. Include observations regarding formation issues and growth as well as evidence for these. Below are examples of evaluations:

N. is faithful to every aspect of the seminary's spiritual life program. The Eucharist, the Sacrament of Reconciliation and the Liturgy of the Hours.

X is faithful to every aspect of the seminary's spiritual life program. He regularly attends and participates in daily liturgy, prays the Liturgy of the Hours, and takes advantage of the Sacrament of Reconciliation. He reports meeting regularly with his spiritual director. His spiritual practice includes ....

Intellectual and Pastoral Development

- Type of student, degree program, GPA for the fall____. Describe any intellectual growth or challenges he experienced during the year.
- Describe last summer's pastoral experience.
- Pastoral experience, including comments from ministry supervisor. Below is a sample of a preaching evaluation:
  This year, ___ is serving at _____Hospital as part of the Basic Supervised Ministry program. (Include comments from Supervisor for Basic.)

Recommendation

The faculty of the seminary commends N. for the many ways he has made use of the opportunities to grow in.... The seminary community appreciates.... The faculty commends or sees potential. Therefore, the faculty recommends...

I have read this evaluation.

I accept it. _____ I do not accept it. _____

Seminarian's
Signature: _____ Date:_____

Advisor's
Signature: _____Date:_____

Pre-Theology

Faculty Evaluation of Paul of Tarsus

Spring, 2016

Paul, a forty-nine-year-old seminarian sponsored by the Diocese of Tarsus, is completing his second year of pre-theology at The Catholic University of America and his second year of formation at Theological College. He has been instituted as a Lector and performs that ministry well. This evaluation will review his formational progress this year and conclude with a recommendation that Paul advance to first theology upon his return to Theological College in the fall.

Human and Spiritual Development

Paul spent the summer at St. Philip's parish in Fairfax. He returned to Theological College excited to be with his friends in the house, return to his classes and the routine of the house. Paul remains an engaging, intelligent and insightful man. He enjoys an honest and open relationship with his advisor. He comes to advising ready to discuss all manner of formation issues. Paul's chief formation goal this year was to integrate and internalize what he learns through the formation process. As he put it, he wants to be a seminarian rather than just act like one. His advisor has watched this change occur in the way he engages formation, takes seriously his studies, prayer life and pastoral ministry. Paul's other goal was to broaden and deepen the ways he engages people in the house beyond superficial conversations. He has made progress towards this goal by becoming aware of his conversations and reflecting on them.

Paul is faithful to every aspect of the seminary's spiritual life program. He regularly attends and participates in daily liturgy, prays the entire Liturgy of the Hours on a daily basis, and takes advantage of the Sacrament of Reconciliation. He reports meeting regularly with his spiritual director and finds that relationship to be a great help to him. His spiritual practices include the rosary, a regular holy hour, and *lectio divina*. He has added the Sulpician Meditation to his set of prayer practices, finding it to be very fruitful. Paul belongs to a *Jesu Caritas* group. His spiritual formation goal for the year was to view his spiritual life as a relationship and not just another task to accomplish.

Intellectual and Pastoral Development

Paul is enrolled in the pre-theology program. Last fall he earned a GPA of 3.60 for a cumulative GPA of 3.743. Paul has worked hard this year to remain organized and on top of his reading and writing assignments with great success. At first, he struggled to adjust to the study of philosophy but his formator encouraged him to pay attention to the questions and issues the philosophers raised. He found this approach to his studies made philosophy more interesting.

Last summer at St. Philip Parish, Paul served at the weekday and weekend liturgies participated in baptisms and funerals, helped with vacation Bible study, and offered adult faith formation lectures on Pope Francis' writings. He learned to adjust to rectory living. He came to love the kindness of the people.

The experience confirmed his vocation to the priesthood. This year, Paul taught catechesis at St. Pius Parish in Bowie Early in the year, Paul discussed with his advisor the challenge of classroom management and pedagogy as he learned to be a catechist. As the year has gone on, he has managed to strike a fruitful balance between guiding class discussion and encouraging student participation with great success.

Recommendation

The faculty of the seminary commends Paul for his open and trusting engagement with the formation program. They see Paul as a bright, intense man who is happy to be at Theological College. Therefore, the faculty recommends that Paul advance to first theology upon returning to Theological College in the fall.

I have read this evaluation.

I accept it. _____ I do not accept it. _____

Seminarian's
Signature: _____ Date:_____

Advisor's
Signature: _____Date:_____

First Theology

Faculty Evaluation of St. Joseph

Spring, 2015

Joseph, a twenty-four-year-old seminarian, sponsored by the Diocese of Nazareth, is completing his first year of theological studies at The Catholic University of America and his first year of formation at Theological College. He has been instituted into the ministries of Lector and Acolyte and performs these ministries well. This evaluation will review his formational progress during the past year and conclude with a recommendation that Joseph return to Theological College in the fall for his second year of theology.

Human and Spiritual Development

Joseph remains a friendly, kind, and intelligent young man. Last summer, Joseph served at St. Andrew Catholic Church in Roanoke. He returned to Theological College excited to study theology and to begin his faith formation ministry at St. John the Baptist parish. In the house, Joseph served as a sacristan and participated in a variety of athletic activities. Joseph enjoys an open and honest relationship with his formator. He came to formation ready to discuss all aspects of the four pillars. Joseph comes across as an easygoing young man. As he moves towards priesthood, his easygoing manner needs to be complemented by an ability to gain deeper insight into his own experiences and those of others. This began to happen for him as he wrestled with the sacrifice involved with celibacy. A friendship with a female student at Catholic University made this very real and personal for him. He discussed this experience with his advisor and his spiritual director. The experience led Joseph to reflect on the importance of boundaries, the question of how to relate to women in a holy and healthy manner, as well as the gift of celibacy. He handled the experience in a mature and open manner which enabled him to continue the friendship while growing in his commitment to celibacy.

Joseph is faithful to every aspect of the seminary's spiritual life program. He regularly attends Eucharist, takes advantage of the Sacrament of Reconciliation and prays the Liturgy of the Hours. He reports meeting regularly for spiritual direction. His spiritual practices include *lectio,* a weekly holy hour, and praying the rosary. During his time in seminary, Joseph has consistently desired to grow closer to the Lord by reading Scripture. During Lent, he devoted himself to reading each of the four Gospels. He has discovered what they have in common and where they differ. He believes this experience has drawn him much closer to the Lord. His newest spiritual formation goal is to create a "spiritual workout plan" similar to a workout regimen in order to remain consistent in his spiritual practices.

Intellectual and Pastoral Development

Joseph is enrolled in the dual STB/M.Div. degree program. Last fall, he earned a 3.90 GPA giving him an overall GPA of 3.875. As is evident from his grades, Joseph is a dedicated and hardworking student who enjoys his studies, especially his Scripture courses. He is discovering a growing desire to deepen how he understands of his faith. In addition, he is finding his studies are helping him talk about the faith and answer questions in his adult faith formation classes

Last summer, Joseph served at St. Andrew in Roanoke where he was exposed to every dimension of parish life. He visited the sick, led a vacation Bible school, and assisted at committals. His pastor/supervisor reported that the parishioners "swarmed" Joseph often inviting him to their home. His supervisor encouraged him to "build on his personal faith with some solid theology." Joseph realized that public speaking will be a big challenge for him. Knowing this, he asked to speak about discerning vocations at his diocesan youth conference. Working with his advisor, Joseph prepared his talk and found the experience very rewarding. This year, he is teaching second grade catechism at St. John the Baptist Catholic Community and conducting an adult education class using Fr. Barron's *Catholicism* series. Joseph has discovered that he enjoys adult education more than youth catechesis. He finds it difficult to gain and keep the attention of the children, whereas the adults are interested and engaged in the material. As of this writing there was no report from his ministry assignment.

Recommendation

The faculty of the seminary commends Joseph for facing head-on the struggles of celibacy. The faculty encourages him to deepen the practice of personal reflection and growth in insight into his own experiences. Therefore, the faculty recommends that Joseph return to Theological College in the fall to begin his second year of formation.

I have read this evaluation.

I accept it. _____ I do not accept it. _____

Seminarian's
Signature: _____ Date:_____

Advisor's
Signature: _____Date:_____

Second Theology

Faculty Evaluation of St. Mark

Spring, 2014

Mark, a twenty-eight-year-old seminarian from the Diocese of Richmond, is completing his third year of priestly formation at Theological College and his second year of theological studies at the Catholic University of America. Instituted as an Acolyte and a Lector, he faithfully fulfills those ministries. This evaluation will review formational progress during the past year and conclude with a recommendation that he be admitted to Candidacy and return to Theological College to continue his formation for priesthood after successfully completing his diocesan mandated pastoral year.

Human and Spiritual Development

Grieving the death of his mother has been a major source of Mark's human development. The shadows of loss have enabled him to develop a greater empathy, be more vulnerable, appreciate more deeply the support and challenge of friends, and become more self-revelatory in the process of formation. He enjoys a wide range of relationships both within and outside the seminary community, using his easygoing nature to enter readily into relationship with others. At the same time, he needs to continue to risk being vulnerable, especially when he finds himself in situations of disagreement with others. As he becomes more comfortable with himself, he is beginning to take those risks that reveal him as a man of depth and integrity.

Mark has the respect of the faculty and an open and honest relationship with his advisor. He is pro-active in the formation process, eager to learn more about himself and about what it means for him personally to be a minister and a man of principle. He is generous in his service to the community, having served as a member of the orientation team, being active in a variety of team sports, and stepping in wherever he is needed for community events. He also volunteers as a server at the Basilica of the National Shrine of the Immaculate Conception. His small group formation facilitator notes that Mark shares appropriately with the group and has demonstrated a deep and concrete appreciation for a life of celibate chastity, the major focus of the small group process for Mark this year.

Eucharist and the Liturgy of the Hours form the core of Mark's spiritual disciplines. While he has sometimes found it difficult to maintain the discipline of praying the Office in its entirety, he is faithful to the practice and has developed a deeper appreciation of the ways in which the psalms resonate with his personal experience of life. He is faithful to the prayer life of the community and has a number of private prayer disciplines that include *lectio divina*, the *examen*, and appropriate Eucharistic and Marian devotions as well as devotion to the saints. The experience of grieving has colored Mark's spiritual development and brought him to a deeper sense of what it means to be a spiritual father, especially as one who accompanies others in love both in sorrows and joys, in peaceful as well as in turbulent times. It has also developed a deeper sense of gratitude in Mark's life. By his own report, he is faithful to spiritual direction and has a good and fruitful relationship with his director. He also regularly receives the sacrament of Penance.

Intellectual and Pastoral Development

While this has been a challenging year for Mark, he feels that he needs to continue to become more disciplined in ensuring a proper balance in his studies to have the leisure to prepare his work in an unhurried manner. He enjoys his studies and has done well in them. He has also developed a greater sense of the importance of his theological studies for the spiritual life and the pastoral ministry. His fall semester GPA was 3.860 giving him a cumulative GPA of 3.725.

Mark is currently assigned to Georgetown Hospital in Washington, D.C., as part of his involvement in the University's program of Basic Supervised Ministry. While Mark often finds himself nervous before beginning his pastoral visits, he has no real hesitation in visiting with patients and finds the process personally rewarding. He feels that he has developed a strong sense of empathy; developed appropriate skills to avoid counter-transferring his interior reactions, especially when visiting cancer patients; and has come to a deep appreciation of the ways in which God acts in times of suffering.

Mark's on-site supervisor notes that he is comfortable and self-confident in his role as pastoral minister, can distinguish between pastoral and social visits, and has begun to appropriately assert his pastoral authority in hospital situations. He notes that Mark relates well with the nursing staff, is proactive in the supervisory process and has developed empathetic and assessment skills. He has explored the issue of his mother's death and its value and hazards for pastoral visits, and seems to be dealing with the issue appropriately. He also commends Mark for his ease in praying with patients.

Mark's group supervisor notes that Mark has developed good active listening skills and demonstrated a flexibility that has enabled him to respond to the needs of patients and their families. He commends Mark for the ways in which his reflection on his mother's death has enabled him to both grieve for her passing and to utilize it in a helpful way in his ministry. He notes that Mark prays easily with others and uses his own attentiveness to his personal affect to pray more effectively with others. He finds that Mark has been able to raise more challenging issues in the group in a manner that allows others to hear them without becoming defensive. Mark himself is very responsive to feedback and seems energized by the group process. While they need to be tightened so that they become more focused, the homilies Mark has shared with his advisor reveal an effective storyteller who communicates his own love for God and for the Church well.

Mark has already developed a number of goals for his pastoral year, including a deepening of his knowledge of Spanish, a desire to shadow the pastor to learn more about the administrative side of ministry, and a desire to participate in the parish's catechetical program. Upon the advice of his vocation director, he will also meet regularly with his advisor. He is looking forward to being totally immersed in the life of the parish and to being engaged full time in ministerial service in it.

Recommendation

The faculty commends Mark for the formational progress he has made this past year, especially for the ways in which he has used his grieving over his mother's death to develop a deeper sense of self and a greater ease in being vulnerable and coming to understand its effective use in the pastoral situation while maintaining appropriate boundaries. They encourage him to continue to develop a deeper appreciation of his many gifts and to grow in confidence. They recommend that he be admitted to Candidacy and look forward to his return to Theological College to continue his formation towards priesthood upon successful completion of his pastoral year.

I have read this evaluation.

I accept it. _____   I do not accept it. _____

Seminarian's
Signature: _____ Date:_____

Advisor's
Signature: _____Date:_____

Third Theology

Faculty Evaluation of St. Augustine

Spring, 2016

Augustine, a thirty-four-year-old seminarian, sponsored by the Archdiocese of Hippo, is completing his third year of theological studies at The Catholic University of America and his third year of formation at Theological College. He has been admitted to Candidacy and instituted into the ministries of Lector and Acolyte. This evaluation will review Augustine's progress during the past year and conclude with a recommendation that he be ordained to the diaconate and return to Theological College to complete his final year of theological studies and formation.

Human and Spiritual Formation

Augustine remains an intelligent, generous, and kind man. During the first half of last summer, he was stationed at Holy Comforter/St. Cyprian parish. Augustine served at the daily and weekend liturgies and offered two communion reflections a week. He also delivered two adult education talks during his time in the parish. During the second half of his summer, Augustine made the Spiritual Exercises at the Broom Tree Retreat Center in South Dakota.

Augustine was happy to return to Theological College after his summer experiences. He comes to advising prepared to discuss issues related to formation with insight, passion, openness, and generosity. Throughout the year, Augustine discussed with his advisor the challenge of balancing the busyness of life in the seminary with his desire to study and be in prayer, the temptation to compare himself to others and letting others have power over him, the need to grow in confidence, and the practice of discerning when to say yes or no when much is asked of him in the house or parish.

Augustine is faithful to every aspect of the seminary's spiritual life program. He regularly attends and participates in daily liturgy, prays the entire Liturgy of the Hours on a daily basis, and takes advantage of the Sacrament of Reconciliation. He is faithful to spiritual direction and is learning to be open with his director. His spiritual practices include the *examen* and *lectio divina*. After his summer experience of the exercises, Augustine found that he is no longer discerning his vocation but preparing for ordination. His experience of the exercises transformed his relationship with Jesus. He now relates to Christ in a personal manner. While on retreat, he discovered the power of praying with Scripture, the beauty of silence, and God's love for him as well as the importance of discerning spirits and the *examen* prayer. These experiences guided Augustine's experience throughout the year. He reports being ready to make the public commitments to celibacy, the Liturgy of the Hours, obedience, and simplicity of life. Augustine understands celibacy to be a unique way for him to remain united to the Lord and give himself fully to God's people in ministry. What drives him is a desire to follow the Lord in freedom which makes him ready to make the promise of obedience to the bishop. He sees simplicity of life as an intentional way of remaining focused on the Lord and his mission.

In the seminary, Augustine serves as the student government treasurer, works part-time in the office on liturgical programs, participates in Social Justice Committee activities, and is heavily involved in the seminary's music program through singing and accompanying liturgies on the piano.

Intellectual and Pastoral Formation

Augustine is studying for the M.Div. and STB degrees. Last fall, he earned a GPA of 3.8 for a cumulative GPA of 3.9. He is preparing to take his comprehensive exams this semester. Augustine is a gifted student who has expressed a desire to go on for further studies. Early in the fall semester, Augustine noticed a change in the way he approaches his course work. While continuing to be a serious student, he no longer views himself as a graduate student but a seminarian whose study is guided by their application to ministry and the spiritual life. Augustine is enrolled in Preaching I and II and is developing the foundations that will make him a good homilist. He is learning the difference between lecturing and preaching, doing more with less, and the power of editing his text. In addition, his experience of the Spiritual Exercises informs how he prays with Scripture and prepares to write a homily.

This year, Augustine served at Holy Redeemer Parish in College Park, Maryland where Fr. Smith is the pastor. Augustine's duties at the parish include serving at weekend liturgies; assisting with youth adult ministry; visiting the School of Religion classes, as well as participating in parish council and other administrative meetings; and attending parish social functions. He enjoys getting to know the people and participating in parish life in preparation for ordination.

Recommendation

The faculty of the seminary commends Augustine for his commitment to the formation program and for the ways he has grown in confidence. They appreciate the many contributions he has made to the community this year. Augustine is a very gifted man with a deep desire to know and serve the Lord. Therefore, the faculty recommends that he be ordained to the diaconate and return to the seminary for his final year of studies and formation.

I have read this evaluation.

I accept it. _____   I do not accept it. _____

Seminarian's
Signature: _____ Date:_____

Advisor's
Signature: _____Date:_____

Fourth Theology

Faculty Evaluation for Reverend Mr. Michael the Archangel

Spring 2014

Michael, a thirty-year-old seminarian sponsored by the Diocese of Pittsburgh, is completing his final year of formation at Theological College and his final year of theological studies at The Catholic University of America. He is an ordained deacon. This evaluation will review his progress during the past year and conclude with a recommendation that he be ordained to the priesthood for service to the people of his diocese.

Human and Spiritual Development

Michael is an engaging, intelligent, organized, and generous seminarian who goes above and beyond in both his service and presence to the seminary community. He has spent a large part of this formation year preparing for his transition back to his diocese as an ordained priest. Michael has made it a point to seek out both spiritual director and support group to help him acclimate to his new life as associate pastor within the diocese. He has been able to look over his four years of formation with gratitude, particularly as it has provided him with numerous opportunities for growth and self-awareness, whether in the form of peer relationships, formation faculty feedback, *Jesu Caritas* group, or diocesan fraternity within the community of Pittsburgh seminarians for whom he feels special gratitude.

Michael has struggled this year between the need to be liked as a minister and the need to set clear boundaries for himself within the context of his parish ministry. As a talented and engaging minister, this struggle will be an ongoing challenge for him—learning how to set boundaries on his time and energy so that he doesn't overextend his availability causing his ministry to suffer as a consequence is essential. Michael is learning the fine balance in this continuum; he feels more comfortable with the balance he has achieved over the year.

Spiritually, Michael has been focused on improving his prayer life, both in terms of quantity and quality. He engages in the following prayer practices: a daily holy hour, all the hours of the office, frequent prayer of the rosary, *lectio divina*, meditative prayer, and spiritual reading. By his own report, he makes regular use of the sacrament of reconciliation. With the aid of his spiritual director, Michael has reflected more deeply upon his priestly identity and has tried to identify ways he can maintain a happy, healthy priestly ministry. He has renewed his commitment to the promises he made in his diaconate ordination and feels well equipped to engage in a lifetime of priestly service.

Intellectual and Pastoral Development

Michael has continued to excel academically in his study of theology. He is well on the way to completing the requirements for his dual M.Div./STB. degree. In the fall semester, he earned a 4.0 GPA which gives him a cumulative GPA of 3.922. Michael has found two courses particularly helpful to his preparation for parish ministry: pastoral counseling and pastoral leadership. These courses have offered him a chance to increase skills such as empathetic listening, assessment, management style, and collaboration. Michael is thankful for the blessing his study at Catholic University has been for him. The faculty recommends that the diocese seriously consider Michael for continuing study because of his solid intellect and excellent academic achievements.

Michael has sought out leadership positions during this diaconal year to help him prepare for the leadership that awaits him in parish ministry. He has served as chair of the Prayer and Worship Committee, a role that he finds directly applicable to his future parish ministry. He has also availed himself of leadership positions within his pastoral placement at St. Matthias parish including training lectors and Eucharistic ministers, conducting a retreat for the Knights of Columbus, teaching RCIA and religion at the school, and performing sacramental ministry including baptisms, holy hours, and preaching.

Michael has experienced some significant difficulty communicating with his pastor during this formation year. Despite being a source of frustration, this difficulty has turned into a learning opportunity for him to see how poor communication on the part of a pastor can affect the entire ministerial atmosphere within a parish community. Michael has sought out the expertise of other parish staff to gain a better understanding of different elements of parish functions such as budgeting, school issues, religious education planning, and maintenance procedures. Michael has also been trying to fine-tune his public presiding style as he looks forward to parish priestly ministry. He is aware that his style in seminary is not the style that he utilizes within the parish.

Michael is sensitive enough to understand the style of a parish and flexible enough to adapt accordingly.

Recommendation

The faculty commends Michael for his consistent generosity of service over his years of formation. They acknowledge his gift of leadership within the seminary community and his concern for the well-being of his brothers and for the spirit of the community. The faculty sees in Michael a man of great generosity, solid intellect, pastoral sensitivity, and zeal for ministry. They recommend that Michael be ordained to the order of presbyter for service in his diocese.

I have read this evaluation.

I accept it. _____ I do not accept it. _____

Seminarian's
Signature: _____ Date:_____

Advisor's
Signature: _____Date:_____

Selected Bibliography

Magisterial and Sulpician Documents on Formation for Priestly Ministry

Vatican Council II. *Optatam totius*. October 28, 1965.
———. *Presbyterorum ordinis*. December 7, 1965.
John Paul II. *Pastores Dabo Vobis*. Washington, D.C. Office for Publishing and Promotion Services, United States Catholic Conference, 1992.
Congregation for the Clergy. *The Gift of the Priestly Vocation: Ratio Fundamentalis Institutionis Sacerdotalis*. December 8, 2016.
Committee on Priestly Formation of the United States Conference of Catholic Bishops. *Program of Priestly Formation*. 5th ed. Washington, D.C.: USCCB Publishing, 2006.
Marks of a Sulpician Seminary. Society of St. Sulpice, Province of the USA, 1994.
Withcrup, Ronald D., PSS, ed. *The Sulpicians: A Tradition of Priestly Formation*. Paris: Society of the Priests of Saint Sulpice, 2013.

Attachment Theory

Ainsworth, Mary, Mary C. Blehar, Everett Watters, and Sally N. Wall. *Patterns of Attachment: A Psychological Study of Strange Situations.* Hillsdale, NJ: Erlbaum, 1978.

Bowlby, John. *A Secure Base: Parent-Child Attachment and Healthy Human Development.* New York: Basic Books, 1998.

Brooks, David. *The Social Animal: The Hidden Sources of Love, Character, and Achievement.* New York: Random House, 2012. See esp. chap. 5, "Attachment."

Cozolino, Louis. *The Neuroscience of Human Relationships: Attachments and the Developing Social Brain.* New York: W. W. Norton, 2006. See esp. chap. 10, "Ways of Attaching."

> Sets out the recent developments in neuroscience for understanding human relationships and attachment. This book is written for people in the helping relationship field.

Lewis, Thomas, Fari Armini, and Lannon, Richard. *A General Theory of Love.* New York: Random House, 2000. See esp. chap. 4, "A Fiercer Sea: How Human Relationships Permeate the Body, Mind and Soul."

> A wonderful introduction to what neuroscience can teach us about relationships.

Siegel, Daniel. *The Mindful Therapist: A Clinicians Guide to Mindsight and Neural Integration.* New York: W. W. Norton and Company, 2010.

> Siegel presents the recent findings of neuroscience and mindfulness for the practice of therapy. Formation advisors have much to learn from his work.

———. *Mindsight: The New Science of Personal Transformation.* New York: Bantam Books, 2011. See esp. chap. 9, "Making Sense of Our Lives: Attachment and the Story Telling Brain."

———. *The Developing Mind: How Relationships and the Brain Interact to Shape Who We Are.* New York: The Guilford Press, 2015.

Celibacy

Aschenbrenner, George, SJ. *Quickening the Fire in Our Midst: The Challenge of Diocesan Priestly Spirituality.* Chicago: Loyola Press, 2002.

Bleichner, Howard, Daniel Buechlein, and Robert Leavitt. *Celibacy for the Kingdom: Theological Reflections and Practical Perspectives.* Rev. ed. Baltimore: St. Mary's Seminary and University, 1990. Criterion Press, 1997.

Congregation for the Clergy. *The Gift of the Priestly Vocation: Ratio Fundamentalis Institutionis Sacerdotalis.* December 8, 2016.

John Paul II. *Pastores Dabo Vobis.* Washington, D.C. Office for Publishing and Promotion Services, United States Catholic Conference, 1992.

Manuel, Gerdenio Sonny, SJ. "Living Chastity; Psychosexual Well-Being in Jesuit Life." *Studies in the Spirituality of Jesuits* 41, no. 2 (Summer 2009).

Paul VI. *Sacerdotalis Caelibatus*: *Encyclical of Pope Paul VI on the Celibacy of the Priest,* June 24, 1967. http://w2.vatican.va/content/paul-vi/en/encyclicals.index.html.

Sacred Congregation for Catholic Education. *A Guide to Formation in Priestly Celibacy*. Rome, 1974.

For the Sake of the Kingdom: A Sulpician Approach to Formation in Priestly Celibacy. Paris: The Society of the Priests of St. Sulpice, 2005.

Vatican Council II. *Presbyterorum ordinis*. December 7, 1965.

Common Formation Issues

Adult Children of Alcohols (Association). *Adult Children of Alcoholics: Alcoholic and Dysfunctional Families*. Torrance, CA: World Service Organization, Inc., 2006.

> The comprehensive text on all the issues adult children face. This book is not just for children from homes of alcoholics. It is filled with great insights into many formation issues formators find seminarians deal with as well as ways to help them.

Bargh, John. *Before You Know It*. New York: Touchstone, 2017.

Blanchette, Melvin, PSS. "Negotiating the Pillars of Formation." An unpublished document.

> A wonderful guide to the various issues a formator should discuss with his advisees at each stage of formation taking into account the four pillars.

Bradberry, Travis, and Jean Greaves. *Emotional Intelligence 2.0*. San Diego, CA: TalentSmart Publishers, 2009.

> This book lays out in simple language the four skills of emotional intelligence: self-awareness, self-management, social awareness, and relationship management. It comes with an online test to

gauge your emotional quotient and examples of high and low skilled people and strategies for growing all four skills.

Brooks, David. *The Social Animal: The Hidden Sources of Love, Character, and Achievement.* New York: Random House, 2012.

An engaging and eye-opening survey of recent insights into relationships and human development from the field of neuroscience.

———. *The Road to Character.* New York: Random House, 2015.

Cain, Susan. *Quiet: The Power of Introverts in a World that Can't Stop Talking.* New York: Broadway Books, 2013.

A ground-breaking book on the power of introverts, silence, solitude, and creativity in a world that privileges extroverts and group brain storming. Very important for advising since many seminarians are introverts.

Dweck, Carol. *Mindset: The New Psychology of Success: How We Can Learn to Fulfill Our Potential.* New York: Ballantine Books, 2006.

Sets out on the impact of a "fixed mindset" compared to a "growth mindset" on various dimensions of life. This book is can help formators promote a growth mindset within the men they guide.

Jay, Meg. *The Defining Decade. Why Your Twenties Matter and How to Make the Most of Them Now.* New York: Twelve, 2013.

An important book for advisors who are working with men in their twenties. Filled with insights into what is happening developmentally at this age and what is needed for them to grow and mature.

Horney, Karen. "The Tyranny of the Should." *Neurosis and Human Growth: The Struggle Toward Self-Realization.* New York: W.W. Norton and Company, reissued in 1991.

———. "Self-Hate and Self-Contempt." *Neurosis and Human Growth: The Struggle Toward Self-Realization.* New York: W.W. Norton and Company, reissued in 1991.

McBrearity, Gerald, PSS. "Spiritual Development." *Seminary News* 32, no. 3 (1994).

Newberg, Andrew. *Words Can Change Your Brain: Twelve Conversation Strategies to Build Trust, Resolve Conflict and Increase Intimacy.* New York: Plume Publishing, 2013.

> Combining the insights of neuroscience and communication studies, these authors offer seminarians twelve strategies for compassionate communication.

Stein, Steven J., and Howard E. Book, MD. *The EQ Edge: Emotional Intelligence and your Success.* Mississauga, ON: Jossey-Bass, 2011.

Culture and Society

Bellah, Robert, Richard Madsen, William M. Sullivan, Ann Swidler, and Steven M. Tipton. *Habits of the Heart: Individualism and Commitment in American Life.* 3rd ed. Berkeley: University of California Press, 2007.

> A now classic study of the origins and meaning of the cultural trend of American individualism

and its implications for education, work, and a life of meaning. This has infected the priesthood and how some men approach formation.

Cavanaugh, William T. *Migrations of the Holy: God, State, and the Political Meaning of the Church*. Grand Rapids: Eerdmans, 2011.

A brilliant analysis of contemporary Western culture that challenges the current understanding of secular culture. Rather than seeing secular culture eclipsing religion and belief, Cavanaugh makes the case that the "holy" has migrated in recent centuries in the minds of Westerners from the God of Christianity to the State and the economy.

Damon, William. *The Path to Purpose: How Young People Find Their Calling in Life*. New York: Free Press, 2008.

Renowned psychologist describes the crisis of meaning impacting our society, especially young people and the importance of helping young people find their calling.

Diangelo, Robin. *White Fragility: Why It's So Hard for White People to Talk about Racism*. Boston: Beacon Press, 2018.

A powerful presentation of the major issues associated with racism by a sociologist who presents racism as a cultural and societal system that promotes the advantages of whites while creating obstacles for people of color. The book is written for white people who do not consider themselves racist but nonetheless benefit from being white.

Massingale, Bryan. *Racial Justice and the Catholic Church*. Maryknoll, NY: Orbis Books, 2010.

> Fr. Massingale offers an eye-opening discussion of racism as a cultural system of meanings and values that gives rise to economic, political, and social advantages for whites and disadvantages for people of color. He analyzes the Church's response to racism and draws on our tradition to present a robust response to this cultural original sin.

Sales, Nancy Jo. *American Girls: Social Media and the Secret Lives of Teenagers*. New York: Penguin Random House, 2016.

> Don't be fooled by the title. This is a very important and shocking study of the social and moral impact of social media on young teens and young adults. It offers real insight into the culture seminarians come from and to which we must preach the Gospel.

Smith, Christian. *Soul Searching: The Spiritual Life of American Teens*. Oxford: Oxford University Press, 2009.

> The first study of the religious life of teens in the United States. The value of this study for seminary formation is how it uncovers the dominant spirituality that is found in teens and their parents. Smith coined the term "Moralistic Therapeutic Deism" to identify the main features of this spirituality.

Smith, James, K. A. *How (Not) to be Secular: Reading Charles Taylor*. Grand Rapids: Eerdmans Publishing, 2014.

> A clear analysis and explanation of our secular culture in the light of Charles Taylor's massive study of the emergence of secular culture in the West. This

is an extremely helpful book for understanding the larger culture context that shapes the worldview of our men and us.

Taylor, Charles. *Modern Social Imaginaries*. Durham, NC: Duke University Press (4th Printing), 2007.

Taylor's historical analysis of the rise of secular culture in the West.

Turkle, Sherry. *Reclaiming Conversation: The Power of Talk in a Digital Age*. New York: Penguin Press, 2015.

A study of the impact our devices have on every area of life: solitude, empathy, family, friendship, education, and work. Two important concerns for formation work are the ways in which technology is undermining empathy and our ability to converse.

Diet, Exercise, and Nutrition

Fuhrman, Joel. *The End of Heart Disease: The Eat to Live Plan to Prevent and Reverse Heart Disease*. New York: HarperOne Books, 2016.

A readable and compelling book on healthy eating.

Fung, Jason. *The Obesity Code: Unlocking the Secrets of Weight Loss*. Berkeley: Greystone Books, 2016.

Perhaps the most important book you will read on nutrition with a focus on the cause of obesity. The book debunks many of our assumptions regarding weight loss and diet including the dominant belief that less calories, less fat, and more exercise leads to weight loss. The book makes a powerful evidence-based claim citing many studies that it is the increase in insulin and insulin resistance that lead to weight gain. The last two chapters offer clear guidelines as to what to eat and when to eat. This is a very valuable book as many seminarians face issues with their weight.

Gilbala, Martin. *The One Minute Workout: Science Shows a Way to Get Fit that is Smarter, Faster, Shorter*. New York: Penguin Random House, 2017.

Dr. Martin Gilbala runs the internationally recognized exercises science program at McMaster University. His research has shown how short intense forms of exercises (10 minutes or less) can achieve the same or better results than forty-five minutes of exercise each day. A very readable and interesting book with simple descriptions of brief exercises that increase strength and wind. He also discusses the many medical benefits his research team found results from high intensity but brief forms of exercise.

Hyman, Mark. *Eat Fat Get Thin: Why the Fat We Eat is the Key to Sustained Weight Loss and Vibrant Health*. New York: Little, Brown, Spark, 2016.

Hyman, a well-known author and doctor at the Cleveland Clinic, turns forty years of diet advice on its head. For years, we have been told fat makes you fat when it turns out there is no scientific evidence to back up this claim. What makes us fat is the consumption of refined carbohydrates that cause a dramatic rise in insulin. The consumption of healthy fat fills us up and does not cause a spike in insulin. This is a very readable book based on the latest research. It comes with list of good food to eat and recipes.

Ludwig, David. *Always Hungry: Conquer Cravings, Retrain Fat Cells, and Lose Weight Permanently.* New York: Grand Central Life & Style, 2016.

>Harvard researcher David Ludwig debunks the belief that eating fat makes us fat while promoting a diet of healthy fats, protein, and carbs that avoids the real dangers of processed foods and refined carbs. The book includes menus and recipes.

Mosely, Michael with Peta Bee. *FastExercise: The Simple Secret of High-Intensity Training.* New York: Atria Books, 2013.

>A practical introduction to the science and practice of brief, effective high intensity exercise with descriptions of different exercises. Perfect for busy people.

Mosely, Michael, and Mimi Spencer. *The FastDiet: Lose Weight, Stay Healthy, Live Longer by Simple Secret of Intermittent Fasting.* Rev. ed. New York: Atria Books, 2015.

>An excellent book on the importance of intermittent fasting for weight loss.

Discernment

Gallagher, Timothy. *The Discernment of Spirits: An Ignatian Guide for Everyday Living.* New York: Crossroad, 2005.

>A practical guide through St. Ignatius of Loyola's first set of rules on discerning spirits. This is a very readable book packed with wisdom about the spiritual life and Ignatian spirituality based on the best

scholarship. Gallagher presents Ignatius "Rules" along with case studies. This is an invaluable text for spiritual directors and advisors.

———. *The Examen Prayer*. New York: Crossroad Publishing, 2006.

Gallagher presents St. Ignatius of Loyola's classic prayer, the *Examen*, in a way that brings it to life by showing how this prayer captures the fundamental features of our relationship with Christ.

———. *Discerning the Will of God: An Ignatian Guide to Christian Decision Making*. New York: Crossroad, 2009.

A clear presentation using case studies of the three Ignatian methods of discerning God's will. An essential text for spiritual directors and advisors who are helping a man discern his vocation.

Hahnenberg, Edward. *Awakening Vocation: A Theology of Christian Call*. Collegeville, MN: Liturgical Press, 2010.

A dense and insightful contemporary theology of vocation drawing on the riches of our Christian tradition.

Evaluation and Bias

Heath, Dan, and Chip Heath. *Decisive: How to Make Better Choices in Life and Work*. New York: Random House, 2013.

Based on the Nobel Prize winning work of Daniel Kahneman and Amos Tversky, this book by the Heath brothers lays out in easy to understand terms the biases at work in our judgments and decisions and how to prevent ourselves from falling prey to them. A very important work for formators who are in the evaluation business!

Kahneman, Daniel. *Thinking Fast and Slow*. New York: Farrar, Straus, and Giroux, 2011.

    The Noble Prize winner's masterpiece on how the human mind works when it makes judgments and decisions.

———. "Judgment under Uncertainty: Heuristics and Bias." Originally published in *Science* 185, no. 4157 (1974): 1124–31. It is now found in Appendix A of *Thinking Fast and Slow*.

———. "Choices, Values, and Frames." Originally published in *American Psychologist* 39, no. 4 (1984): 341–350. It is now found in Appendix B of *Thinking Fast and Slow*.

Lewis, Michael. *The Undoing Project: A Friendship that Changed Our Minds*. New York: W.W. Norton and Company, 2017.

    Lewis presents the story of the Israeli soldiers and psychologists Amos Tversky and Daniel Kahneman's friendship and collaboration as they unveiled the many hidden biases in our decisions and transformed the science of decision-making and evaluation.

Forming the Heart and Imagination

Smith, James K. A. *Desiring the Kingdom: Worship, Worldview and Cultural Formation,* Volume 1. Grand Rapids: Baker Academic, 2009.

———. *Imagining the Kingdom: How Worship Works*, Volume 2. Grand Rapids: Baker Academic, 2013.

———. *You are What You Love: The Spiritual Power of Habit.* Grand Rapids: Brazos Press, 2016.

>Philosopher and theologian, Smith presents a vision of the human person that gives priority to the heart and imagination rather than the intellect. Smith develops this vision of the human person with formation and liturgy in mind. He offers the conceptual background to the work of formation advising.

Olthuis, James H. *The Beautiful Risk: A New Psychology of Loving and Being Loved.* Grand Rapids: Zondervan, 2001.

Weddell, Sherry. *Forming Intentional Disciples: The Path to Knowing and Following Jesus.* Huntington, IN: Our Sunday Visitor, 2012.

>Weddell's book presents an approach to forming Christians who live from a relationship with Christ in the Christian community. Her book presents five stages that lead to intentional discipleship. This book offers formators a way to identity where on this journey to discipleship the men with whom they work may be. It also helps us understand what a person needs at each stage.

Wright, N. T. *Surprised by Hope: Rethinking Heaven, the Resurrection and the Mission of the Church.* New York: HarperOne Publishing, 2008.

———. *Simply Good News: Why the Gospel is News and What Makes It Good.* New York: HarperOne Publishing, 2014

———. *Surprised by Scripture*. New York: Harper One Publishing, 2014.

Listening

Barry, William A., and William Connolly. *The Practice of Spiritual Direction*. 2nd rev. and updated ed. New York: HarperOne, 2009.

> A classic in spiritual direction with an emphasis on listening to the experience of the person. A must for spiritual directors and very helpful for advisors.

Guenther, Margaret. *Holy Listening: The Art of Spiritual Direction*. Cambridge, MA: Cowley Publications, 1992.

> A classic from the field of spiritual direction with wonderful insights into the art of listening every advisor can benefit from reading.

Kimsey-House, Henry, Karen Kimsey-House, and Philip Sandahl, and Whitworth, Laura. *Co-Active Coaching: Changing Business, Transforming Lives*. 3rd ed. Boston: Nicholas Brealy Publishing, 2011.

> An important text from the field of leadership coaching that provides a powerful model for working with people that advisors could really benefit from.

Newberg, Andrew. *Words can Change Your Brain: Twelve Conversation Strategies to Build Trust, Resolve Conflict and Increase Intimacy*. New York: Plume Publishing, 2013.

Perhaps the book I would give to a new formator. Combining the insights of neuroscience and communication studies, these authors offer formators twelve strategies for compassionate communication.

Parish Life and Leadership

Byron, William J., SJ. *Parish Leadership: Principles and Practices.* Lakewood, NJ: Clear Faith Publishing, 2017.

Jesuit William Byron discusses the importance of shared leadership as servant leadership rather than the corrupting to down approach. He also discusses the importance of introducing Catholic Social Teaching into parish life.

Heath, Chip, and Dan Heath. *Switch: How to Change Things When Change is Hard.* New York: Broadway Books, 2010.

The Heath brothers bring together years of research in a story-driven narrative about how cultures, institutions, and persons can change. Formators can learn a great deal from this book about the process of guiding seminarians to make the changes needed in formation.

Kouzes, James M., and Barry Z. Posner. *The Leadership Challenge: How to Make Extraordinary Things Happen in Organizations.* 5th ed. San Francisco: Jossey-Bass, 2012.

Mallon, James. *Divine Renovation: Bringing Your Parish from Maintenance to Mission.* New London, CT: Twenty-Third Publications, 2014.

Roxburgh, Alan J., and Fred Romanuk. *The Missional Leader: Equipping Your Church to Reach a Changing World.* San Francisco: Jossey-Bass, 2006.

Sipp, James W., and Don M. Frick. *Seven Pillars of Servant Leadership: Practicing the Wisdom of Leading by Serving.* Mahwah, NJ: Paulist Press, 2015.

Simon, William E. *Great Catholic Parishes: A Living Mosaic —How Four Essential Practices Make Them Thrive.* Notre Dame, IN: Ave Maria Press, 2016.

White, Michael. *Rebuilt: Awakening the Faithful, Reaching the Lost, and Making Church Matter.* Notre Dame, IN: Ave Maria Press, 2013.

> White, a priest from the Archdiocese of Baltimore, tells the story of bringing a dying parish back to life and transforming it into a parish that matters to people's lives. An essential read for all fourth-year seminarians.

———. *Tools for Rebuilding: 75 Really, Really Practical Ways to Make Your Parish Better.* Notre Dame, IN: Ave Maria Press, 2013.

> The follow up to *Rebuilt*. This book is filled with wonderful and concrete suggestions for bringing our parishes to life.

Preaching

Heath, Chip, and Dan Heath. *Made to Stick: Why Some Ideas Survive and Others Die.* New York: Random House, 2008.

> These authors present a tested method for developing a message that sticks to the imagination of

people. These authors advocate for SUCCES: Simple, Unexpected, Concrete, Clear, Emotional Stories approach to presentations. Every preacher should read this book.

McCormack, Deacon Edward. "Ten Commandments for Transformative Preaching." *Homiletic & Pastoral Review* (http:/www.hprweb.com/). November 29, 2015.

A concrete guide to preaching in a way that connects Scripture to the lives of the people in order to promote transformation.

Stanley, Andy, and Lane Jones. *Communicating for a Change*. Colorado Springs: Multnomah Books, 2006.

This may be the most important book any seminarian reads about preaching. The authors propose as the goal of preachers transformation rather than information. With this goal in mind, Stanley and Lane direct preachers to pick one message and build their homily around it using a relational model of preaching. This model starts with where the people are, interprets that situation through Scripture, and concludes by showing how to put the message into practice.

Untener, Kenneth. *Preaching Better: Practical Suggestions for Homilists*. Mahwah, NJ: Paulist Press, 1999.

A classic that covers the fundamentals of preparing and delivering a homily. Each chapter begins with wisdom from the people who listen to our preaching. It is a gold mine!

Wallace, James. *Preaching to the Hungers of the Heart: The Homily on the Feasts and within the Rites*. Collegeville, MN: Liturgical Press, 2002.

Written by a master professor of homiletics, this book offers practical wisdom for anyone preaching with special attention to feast days, various church seasons, Mary, and the sacraments.

Priesthood

Aschenbrenner, George, SJ. *Quickening the Fire in Our Midst: The Challenge of Diocesan Priestly Spirituality.* Chicago: Loyola Press, 2002.

Based on Aschenbrenner's experience as a spiritual director at the North American College and founder of IPF, this book describes the different dimensions of diocesan spirituality that can be very helpful for seminarians.

Buckley, Michael. "Importance of Weakness in the Priesthood: A Letter to the Ordinands [Jesuits about to be Ordained]." *The Berkeley Jesuit* (Spring 1972): 8.

Congar, Yves. *A Gospel Priesthood.* Translated by P. J. Hepburne-Scott. New York: Herder and Herder, 1967.

Chapters 6, 8, 9, 10, and 11 offer a goldmine of insights into the priesthood from one of our great theologians.

Hahnenberg, Edward P. *Ministries: A Relational Approach.* New York: Herder & Herder, 2003.

An important theological study of ordained ministry. In critical dialogue with the tradition and building on the insights of Vatican II, the work proposes that ordained ministry be set within the context of the Christian community and seen as a permanent and public commitment to service to that community. What changes for the ordained is his relationship to the community and the public and permanent service he offers that community. The book contains rich and practical insights for ordained ministry.

Rolheiser, Ronald. *Sacred Fire: A Vision for a Deeper Human and Christian Maturity.* New York: Random House, 2014.

Written by a master of the spiritual life, Rolheiser sets out the spiritual life in terms of three moments in human development: the effort to get our lives together; the challenge of giving our lives away; and finally, giving our deaths away. Rolheiser draws on Scripture and the wisdom of the Christian spiritual tradition to describe these three movements. This book is filled with rich insights into the spiritual life that are particularly relevant to seminary formation since that process compresses the first two moments and challenges the men to move into and through both as they head towards ordination.

Index

advising meetings, 63-95; celibacy, 74-81; discipleship 90-95; discussing transitions, 69-72; emotional intelligence, 85-88; getting to know the seminarian, 45-48, 68-69; human formation issues, 81-85; listening, 43-45, 66-68; pastoral skill development, 88-90; preparing seminarians for meetings, 132-33.

accompaniment, 3, 29-37, 63-94; caring approach, 36-38; and deep listening, 119-23; skills, 41-43; throughout the year, 53-56; two forms, 29-32

annual evaluation, writing the, 150-58; evaluation guide, 152-56; first theology, 165-68; fourth theology, 178-81; pre-theology, 162-64; sample evaluations, 159-81; second theology, 169-73; style sheet, 151; third theology, 174-77; trouble shooting, 156-58

attachments, 38-41, 85-86, 111, 184-85

Bargh, John (*Before You Know It*), 109, 113-16, 135-36

bias, 82, 142-46, 194-95; stereotypes, 112, 114, 145

celibacy, 74-81

character formation, 27, 111-12, 187

childhood. *See* heart

communication, 49, 188, 198; intercultural, 51-53, 73-74, 188-89

conflict, 20n23, 52, 74-75, 197-98

consumer culture, 46, 77, 103-06

contexts of formation, 19-22; ecclesial context, 22; historical and cultural, 19-21; multicultural, 19, 51-53; seminary community, 23

discernment, 26, 32, 65, 75-76, 193-94; pastoral, 13, 90, 94

discipleship, 13, 17-19, 25-26, 90-95, 99-100, 117-18, 196

Dweck, Carol (*Mindset*), 126-28, 187

emotions. *See* advising meetings

evaluation, 141-82; bias in evaluations, 142-46; fall review, 146; guiding the seminarian self-evaluation, 149-50; pre-evaluation conversation, 147-49; writing the annual evaluation, 150-58

fasting, 193

formation, 7-16; characteristics of, 13-14; contexts of- 17-22; dimensions, 10-12; intellectual, spiritual, and pastoral issues, 56-61; principles of, 15-16

formation advising, 32-37, 64-66; attachments, 38-41; caring approach, 36-38; feedback, 48-50; forming the heart and imagination, 98-107; intercultural communication, 51-53; listening, 43-45; note taking, 50-51; questions, 45-48; skills, 41-43

formation, fundamental features of, 25-28

formation issues, 54-61, 186-88; beginning of the year, 54-55, human formation, 57-58; intellectual formation, 60; pastoral formation, 61; spiritual formation, 59-60; spring semester, 55; throughout the year, 55-56; trust, 32, 36-38, 84, 88 formation, process of, 7-9; addressing wounds, 25, 81, 84; characteristics of formation, 13-15; dimensions of formation, 10-13; principles of formation 15-17; stages of priestly formation, 8-9

formator, 23-25

friendships, 88

heart, 97-122; deeper listening, 98-103, 119-23; deep world within, 107-10; formed and deformed, 103-07; heart and imagination, 98-103; hidden future, 115-17; hidden past, 110-12; hidden present, 112-15; implications for formation, 117-19

imagination, 98-103, 195-97.

intercultural communication. *See* communication

internal and external forum, 30-32

Jesus Christ: center of life and priesthood, 13; center of the universe, 118; death and resurrection, 34, 78, 118-19; and his disciples, 33-34; Good Shepherd, 5, 10, 12, 17, 24, 67, 80-82, 93-95, 97; images of, 120; and Mary, 18; relationship with, 9, 11, 17, 25-26, 91-93, 175, 194; Servant, 9, 25-27, 67, 82, 93-94; as true formator, 23-24, 125

Kimsey-House, Henry (*Co-Active Coaching*), 44-47, 197

mission, 8, 15, 16

parish ministry, 61, 71-72, 81-82, 89-90, 137, 167, 174, 176, 178-80, 198-99

participation, 125-40; goal setting process, 133-34; growth mindset, 126-130; implementing good habits, 134-36; pastoral practice, 137-38; preparing for advising meetings, 132-33; reflection on preaching, 138-39; regular reflection, 130-31; self-evaluation, 139-40

Pastores Dabo Vobis, 4n1, 8n1, 10, 23-24, 78n8,

80n11
Pope Francis, xiii, 25-26, 125
preaching, 60-61, 71-72, 73, 86, 90, 115, 128-131, 138-39, 199-201
Ratio Fundamentalis Formationis Sacerdotalis, xiv-xv, 4n1, 8-15, 19n21, 23-28, 29-30, 32n5, 54, 68n1, 85n13, 93-95, 125, 130n2, 141n1
review. *See* evaluation
Scripture, 12, 18, 60, 105, 200; and prayer, 59, 134, 166, 175-76, 202
servant-leadership, 82, 94, 198. *See also* Jesus Christ
Siegel, Daniel, 36-38, 40-41, 184
skills, 41-53; listening, 43-45, 197-98; note taking, 50; offering feedback, 48-50; questions, 45-48; variety of, 41-43
Smith, James K. A., 21n25, 99-104, 119n34, 190-91, 195-96
stereotypes. *See* biases
temptation, 135-36
Witherup, Ronald, PSS, xiii-xv, 15n19, 77n5

www.ingramcontent.com/pod-product-compliance
Lightning Source LLC
Chambersburg PA
CBHW030254010526
44107CB00053B/1713